BE
WITH
ME
ALWAYS

BE
WITH
ME
ALWAYS

Essays

RANDON BILLINGS NOBLE

University of Nebraska Press | Lincoln and London

© 2019 by Randon Billings Noble

Acknowledgments for the use of previously
published material appear on pages 167–68, which
constitute an extension of the copyright page.

Figure in "A Pill to Cure Love"
is from Wikimedia Commons.

Publication of this volume was assisted by a grant from the
Friends of the University of Nebraska Press.

Library of Congress Cataloging-in-Publication Data
Names: Noble, Randon Billings, author.
Title: Be with me always: essays /
Randon Billings Noble.
Description: Lincoln: University of Nebraska Press, 2019. |
Includes bibliographical references.
Identifiers: LCCN 2018017691
ISBN 9781496205049 (pbk.: alk. paper)
ISBN 9781496213686 (epub)
ISBN 9781496213693 (mobi)
ISBN 9781496213709 (pdf)
Subjects: LCSH: Noble, Randon Billings. | Near-death
experiences. | Déjà vu. | Memory. | Life change events.
Classification: LCC PS3614.O248 A6 2019 |
DDC 814/.6—dc23
LC record available at https://lccn.loc.gov/2018017691

Set in Whitman by Mikala R. Kolander.
Designed by L. Auten.

Be with me always—take any form—
drive me mad! only *do* not leave me in
this abyss, where I cannot find you!

Heathcliff to Cathy, *Wuthering Heights*

Contents

I

Whatever Bed

The Split

It began one day at the shore. It was late in the summer, right after a hurricane, when the waves were brutal but we swam anyway—throwing our slight selves again and again at the bulk and force of the water. I can't remember what the weather was like, but I imagine it was a hot, clear, fierce day. I was fifteen years old. I was with my best friend.

We drifted farther and farther out until our toes gently left the sand and the salt lifted us up and over each incoming swell. But then one wave rose larger than the rest and picked Jocelyn up (or was it me?) and brought her crashing down on top of me (or was it her?) and slammed us, a tangle of arms and legs, to the bottom, where the impact split us apart. I remember groping toward the surface, feeling the desperation tight in my lungs, and plowing my face deep into the sand—I had lost my sense of direction. There in the ocean's bed, hands clutching fistfuls of shells and weed, I had a long moment of deep clarity. Instead of being taken away, my breath was given back; my panic dissolved into a deep calm, and I hung in suspension with my body.

But this moment was torn from me as a hand, her hand, reached blindly through the dark water, touched my ankle, and, finding, pulled. She reeled me to the surface as a lifeguard reeled her. He had seen us caught in a riptide, had swum out to bring us back, had found her wrist just as she found my ankle, and pulled us both to shore. I remember coughing on the wet sand, the sun and sky piercingly bright, coughing and coughing, faintly realizing that I had lost that moment of clarity in the turbulence of recovery, in my body's mechanics. As I looked over to Jocelyn, I thought I saw a flicker of recognition. We trudged to our towels, embarrassed, and lay in silence. It wasn't until the long drive home up the Jersey Turnpike, in the safety of the car and the dark and the miles we had put behind us, that she said, "We could have died."

I never asked her what she had felt under the waves and never knew if she, too, had a moment of clarity on the threshold of death. I could not have described that moment to her, nearly impossible to put words to, and yet, at the same time, it was the truest thing I had ever—almost—known. What I caught that day was only a glimpse. It would be years before I had another chance to see.

I was in France, at a party, with friends and friends of friends. We were on the patio of someone's country house, playing a drinking game that involved reciting limericks and drawing on each other's faces with a burnt cork. When I went inside for a glass of water, and to take a break from the smoke in my eyes and the French in my head, Marc kissed me behind the pantry door and asked me to go upstairs with him. I said no. But when Enzo, at one in the morning, asked if I wanted to go for a ride on his motorcycle, I said yes.

We flew, no helmets, my hair streaming, the wind blowing any words we might have said into the night behind us. Then I saw the tree ahead of us, and when I knew we couldn't hold the curve, when the impact was inevitable, I thought, with a directness that surprised me, *You should be thinking something really important right now.* But there was no time to think. We slid along a barbed wire fence, crashed into the tree, and I was thrown from the bike. Then nothing.

I came to in a field of grass, its itchiness a reassurance that I was alive. There was, as yet, no need for last thoughts. Instead, I had to attend a more practical need: my arms and legs could move, my head could turn, but my face was wet and I couldn't see out of my left eye. But even while I was absorbed in this physical self, some other part of me stood by, aloof, watching and waiting, for what I didn't know.

"I will get help," Enzo said, stumbling and backing away from me. He tore the motorcycle from the wires of the fence. "I will bring help," he said again, before the engine caught and drowned my weak voice saying over and over, like the lover I wasn't but wanted to be: "Wait. Don't leave me. Wait." Then I was alone—or thought I was. It was dark and getting cold.

That other self grew more vigilant after Enzo left. It watched as I flailed weakly against circumstance. It watched as I dug a mirror out of my back pocket and saw that the wetness on my face was blood—blood had blinded my left eye—and I saw that I wasn't going to be all right after all. It watched as my shock became panic in the privacy of the night fields. But the whimpering, squealing me knew that second self, calm and clear, was there as well, attending me during those moments of separation.

Later I began to wonder if the body has a chemical, something like adrenaline, that bathes us in this calm acceptance. Something different from the endorphins that gauze over our feelings of pain, something instead that gives a mental awareness in the midst of the body's trauma. That day with Jocelyn, underwater, my breath was failing fast. Very little time was left. And that night on the motorcycle there was nothing I could do to prevent the crash, no use for fight or flight. In neither case did I feel pain, but I felt something far deeper, something the essayist Montaigne described after his own terrible accident, five centuries before my own.

Montaigne says nothing of pain but languishes over the pleasure of letting himself go, "that sweet feeling that people have who let themselves slide into sleep." He is so removed from his body—"dead," he claims, "for two full hours"—that these mysteries can be revealed. He describes the "easy and quiet" feeling he had while in the early stages of shock but only hints at the idea of a split. Reading Montaigne a few years after my accident, I began to wonder if during such moments of bodily crisis we split for spiritual reasons. More and more I believe we do.

Before I had left for France, I put on a necklace my godmother had given me when I was a child—a tiny silver cross. As a child, I had been infatuated with stories from the Bible, but as I grew older, I questioned, and by the time I was thirteen, I couldn't go through with the confirmation ceremony, couldn't stand up in front of the congregation and lie about what I wasn't sure I believed. So it was a fear of flying rather than faith that led me to hook the chain around my neck before I boarded the plane to Paris.

The plane, however, landed without incident, and I tucked the cross into my collar. I forgot about it in the weeks that followed until I found myself alone and scared, near a tree by the side of a road laced with barbed wire. I had already seen my bloodied face in the mirror, and my reflection had shocked me out of shock. I couldn't deny that I was hurt; I couldn't pretend that I would leave this place unscarred. Something irrevocable had happened, and still I fought against it. I was desperate to hold onto something, and without thought my hand reached for the cross around my neck.

It is hard in moments of great fear not to reach for a benevolent unknown. Madeleine L'Engle, author of *A Wrinkle in Time*, says that although she cannot intellectually believe in God, she finds it impossible to live as though she does not. I, too, reverted to what seemed a muscle memory. I reached for my throat, to grab onto the cross and all the centuries of meaning it symbolized—but it was gone.

Now, I thought, I am truly alone. And that's when the wave of hysteria I had so carefully been riding broke over me. That's when I split. Half of me twisted my head from side to side—and cried against my helplessness. But there was another part of me that felt distinctly separate, standing next to or above me, watching. I could feel her calm and faint disapproval. Not so much disapproval but wisdom. *You're only making it worse*, my other seemed to say. *There's nothing you can do. There's no one here to hear you. Don't you feel silly, carrying on like this all by yourself?* And although I knew she was right, I couldn't stop until I had cried myself out.

I became unmoored. My body slipped further away. Again, I felt the same calm, the same clarity, I had felt underwater. It was indeed a "sweet feeling," and I remember turning toward it. Did my second self reach down to collect me? Did the two of us become one again but on a plane apart from the physical? The only bright light I saw were the twin beams of headlights. A car stopped for me, its family piled out and held my hands, patted my cheeks, and insisted that I stay conscious until the ambulance arrived.

In the hospital, surrounded by nurses and doctors and two carloads of people from the party, I felt entirely alone. My courage had left me, but my second self had too. After an X-ray, the doctors started firing French at each other so rapidly I couldn't follow. One started feeling my skull, and I grew panicky at the thought of a head injury. But in the wind-whipped snarls of my hair, the doctor's fingers found the cross that had been ripped from my neck; its silver shape had shown up bright white, nearly miraculous, on the film. The next day I would find a tiny cross-shaped bruise on my collarbone; perhaps the moment of impact had pressed it there, or maybe the barbed wire swept the cross up and away to catch in my hair. But there on the hospital gurney I only had a moment to realize that it had been there the whole time, out of reach of my seeking fingers but there just the same, and that I didn't have a brain injury, only three deep lacerations on my face, which now seemed to catch fire as a hand pressed a square of alcohol-soaked gauze to my cheek. I screamed at the wash of pain, shrunk back from the stinging pricks of anesthetic, cried at the deep puncture of each stitch, and whimpered in French, asking again and again when this would be over. Eventually it was, and I was taken "home" to sleep on a crisp white pillow that in the morning would be spotted with blood, which I saw, before the pain, as the first evidence of the trial I had been through the night before.

In the days that followed I spent my mornings on the couch numbing myself with French game shows, surprised that after a week I could solve some of the puzzles on *Wheel of Fortune*. In the afternoons I sat for hours at the piano, unable to read bass clef without A-C-E-G, struggling to pick out the tune to "Für Elise." What I couldn't figure out, though, was what, exactly, had happened. I remembered being proud that my last thought wasn't a knee-jerk *Oh, God*—or worse, *Oh, shit*—but *You should be thinking something really important right now*. I tried to give myself an extra ten seconds before the crash, to move the fence and the tree back fifty feet, to widen the arc of the curve we didn't make—anything to think of that important thing—but I couldn't.

Back in the States I turned to Sherwin B. Nuland's book *How We Die* to try to get some answers about the "state of apparent tranquility and release" that many people enter when threatened with serious trauma or imminent death. Nuland, a doctor and a scientist, is reluctant to ascribe a spiritual dimension to the body's methods, but he speculates that there is "far more at work here than the well-known 'fight or flight' of a rush of adrenaline." Nuland believes that endorphins are the cause of this tranquil state, but he explores their etymology in a way that makes me reconsider their role in the emergence of the split self: "They are *endogenous morphine*-like compounds. *Endogenous* [is] adapted from the Greek *endon*, meaning 'within' or 'inner,' and *gennao*, meaning 'I produce.'" So endorphins are produced by the self within the self. Could the split self be a manifestation of spirit, launched from within our own bodies to help usher us from fear to calm, from life to death?

Even if the split self is triggered by a chemical reaction, it serves no larger, physical, evolutionary purpose. Adrenaline gives us the strength or speed or sureness to survive; our genes have a better chance of being flung into the future. But the moment of clarity the split self gives us is a purely internal gift that affects no one else but the self. And I begin to wonder if that isn't part of the plan as well, if we don't carry a small piece of mystery within us that is intentionally inaccessible for most of our physical, sandwich-eating, bus-riding, everyday lives.

Being in this moment is like lazy Saturday mornings spent in bed—awake yet not fully aware, entranced by the blank expanse of ceiling above, lingering in deep thought that vanishes as soon as I go vertical, leaving nothing but a feeling of great potential behind. This feeling lingers the same way the ghost of the split self does. It is something we can carry with us, regardless of what happens when our split selves reunite, when we get up from whatever bed we have been lying in, and walk back into life.

Mirror Glimpses

I.

Mirrors, which seemed magical in their properties, . . .
were composed of only two primary materials:
a plane of glass pressed up against a plane of silver . . .
When a mirror was broken, the glass could be replaced.
When a mirror grew old, it only had to be resilvered.
It could go on and on. It could go on forever.

Carol Shields, "Mirrors"

Over the sink in the bathroom of my grandparents' summerhouse on the Jersey Shore was a smallish round mirror, and directly opposite it, over the toilet, was a medicine cabinet with a mirrored door. These two mirrors reflected endless images of myself when I stood between them. I tried to see into infinity with these mirrors. It was too blurry.

The small round mirror across from the medicine cabinet was wreathed in wooden roses. The face that looked back at me from this mirror was also round and rosy, framed at the top by a precise line of straight-cut bangs. My eyes were wide and dark, unshadowed by disappointment or compassion. My teeth were new and awkward, the two front ones serrated at the bottom like a bread knife, but I was too young to try to smile with my lips closed or laugh behind my hand. I never thought this face would change. I thought my childhood would go on forever.

Instead, I grew out my bangs and grew up.

Over the sink in the bathroom of the hotel room was a large flat mirror that spanned the length of the wall. Directly opposite it was the shower with its skimpy cloth curtain that somehow managed to block the shower's spray. Everything in the room was cold and white—the tiles, the curtain, the walls, the lights.

The face that looked back at me from this mirror was round and blotchy, framed by a white towel wrapped around my wet hair. The skin below my eyes was puffy and dark, shadowed from tossing and turning on scratchy hotel sheets, and my shower had done little to revive me. My mouth was closed, tight at the corners, wondering what the day would bring.

That afternoon I would start my first day at college, four states away from the place I called home. I tried to spy the future in my reflection, but my eyes were too dark to see anything in them.

Over the four sinks in the bathroom of my dorm were four square mirrors bolted to the wall. Fluorescent lights flickered and buzzed from the ceiling, and a steady drip came from the third shower stall. The face in the mirror was always turning away, on its way to something else; the mirror was too scratched to really see anything anyway.

Every morning I showered early and then twisted my hair into a braid that nearly reached my waist. By late October my damp braid froze on my way to my early-morning French class, and when I returned to my room, I unraveled its crispy kinks to let them dry. When my mom came to pick me up in December, I told her that I had made straight A's but that I felt like nothing existed below my brain stem. My body had become a cup to carry around my brain.

II.

When I was a child, I spake as a child, I understood as a child,
I thought as a child: but when I became a man, I put away
childish things. For now we see through a glass, darkly;

> but then face to face: now I know in part;
> but then shall I know even as also I am known.

1 Corinthians 13:11–13

I knew that I would leave X that night. Our affair had been just that: an affair, not a relationship. But before I met up with him at the bar, I had dinner with a friend at the Odeon. I was dressed up for something else—a Christmas party at work perhaps—and my heels clicked on the tile floor of the bathroom. I caught a glimpse of someone in the mirror, and in a split second my brain thought, *She looks like a woman.* She was wearing a black sheath dress and had her hair swept up in a smooth twist. In the second half of that split second I realized, *Wait—that's me.*

Was I surprised by my own reflection because I was wearing a dress instead of my usual jeans? Or had something happened as a result of the decision I had made to end my affair? I was no longer a girl playing with romance; I looked like a woman.

That night I broke off my affair, and the next day I made the long drive to my parents' house. In the boredom of crossing three states on Route 95, I remembered my first thought when I saw my reflection— "She looks *like* a woman," not "She is a woman." Funny how I had used the word *like.* Maybe I still had some growing up to do.

I did. I only thought I had ended my affair that night. It would take me three more months to make it final. What I caught that night in the mirror at the Odeon was only a glimpse of the woman I would become. I wasn't her yet. I only knew in part.

III.

Vanity comes through Middle English, Old French, and Latin;
through *vanitas* from *vanus*, meaning "empty."

Yoga class. In a room full of mirrors it's almost impossible not to look at yourself. E looks at herself all the time. She's maybe forty, beautiful in a careful yet exotic way, perfectly turned out in tights and a tank top, always a different combination but always some shade of blue. In a conversation her eyes slide off your face to her own, over your shoulder, behind you, reflected by one of the ever-present mirrors. I fight this urge, which is another form of vanity: not to appear vain.

But when doing the poses, I look—greedily—at myself. I bought tights and a tank top of my own to better see what my body looks like. This, however, isn't vanity. It's stunted curiosity. I don't *know* what I look like. I haven't known for some time.

That spring, when the biopsy results came back bad, I was so angry at my body for betraying me that I wanted to divorce it. But since I couldn't, I ignored it. It reminded me of my first year of college, when I was so consumed with studying that my body felt like a big cup to carry around my brain. March and April felt like a return to that. I dressed up to teach, put on lipstick for Wednesday morning meetings—but none of that had anything to do with *me*. It was all just keeping up my former image, behind which I hid.

I never looked down when I changed my clothes or took a bath (before baths were forbidden), I never "took stock" of myself in my full-length mirror. I was in denial of my own physical existence. All the compliments X had given me (thrilled by everything his eyes and hands encountered) evaporated. I became an alien to myself. An alien in my own skin.

After the surgery, after I realized that I was indeed going to live, I started trying to reclaim myself—my physical self, my body. This was slow going. I thought I would relish my first bath: I didn't. I was repulsed by the sight of the body that had insistently occupied my peripheral vision. I still didn't want any part of it. Dr. D prescribed yoga classes as a way of getting mind and body back together. After only two weeks of these classes, it started to work.

Sure, I "inhabit" the poses, I'm conscious of my thoughts and breath, but it's the mirror that's really doing it. I *see* myself—the internal self within my external self—and for the most part I like what I see. But it's more than liking (long lines, light skin that turns pink wherever I'm spending energy, dark eyes, a kind of grace); it's *recognizing*. I *am* that. We are the same thing, "that" and me. I am—in all senses of the phrase—full of myself.

IV.

Mirror comes from the Latin *mirari*, "to wonder."

I used to play a game with myself called "Get to Know Your Profile." I'd stand in front of my bathroom mirror with a hand mirror and tilt my head, talk, chew—all in an effort to see myself as others saw me. I didn't realize how often—when I'm writing, for instance—I get up and look at myself in a mirror until I was at my first writing residency. My studio had no mirror. Instead, I'd catch a glimpse of myself in my computer screen whenever it went dark to save power. It was as if I were checking in to see if I was still there.

In the documentary film *Playing the Part* the filmmaker and narrator Mitch McCabe practices phototherapy. During a difficult time she takes a series of self-portraits, and as we see them flash on the screen, her voice-over tells us that she took these photographs to "get some perspective on things and let me know that I wasn't alone." Is that what I was doing, trying to feel less alone? And what is a mirror but a temporary self-portrait?

V.

We use the expression "look *into* a mirror,"
as though it were an open medium, like water.

Carol Shields, "Mirrors"

The verb *to reflect* comes from the Latin *flectere*, meaning "to bend."

In my bedroom there is a closet with two mirrored doors. Each folds out like a sharp elbow, and my reflection slips away and disappears as the doors slide open. Sometimes, if I don't close them completely, the doors bump out just an inch into the room and I can walk up to them like Dracula and never see my reflection. Only when I am very close can I see my shoulders or maybe an arm, but the bulk of me is invisible within the seam. It's unnerving.

If the doors are half-closed, the angle adds five extra inches to my width. My waist thickens, and one leg nearly doubles. I'm less worried about looking fat than I am about not looking the way I think I look. It's like having a mistaken identity. My outsides don't match up with my expectations.

When I am at work, just before I walk into my classroom, I often stop in a bathroom to check my reflection. The light is institutional, ungenerous. It reveals the shadows under my eyes, the blotch on my cheek, the bright red capillaries threading through the whites of my eyes. Is this what I really look like? I teach my class with this image in mind.

But then after class I might stop in the same bathroom. This time the shadows under my eyes might be lit with exhilaration, the blotch on my cheek hidden by a flush, my eyes bright with success. When did my face change?

We are always trying to claim our fleeting image. Like Narcissus on the riverbank, we strain to see ourselves, but there's always a ripple of distortion, sometimes in our mirror image, sometimes in our memory of it. Usually we are pulled away from this reflection and hustled back into life. But if we linger by the river and reach into the water to catch ourselves, we break up entirely.

Time and time again we have to learn that our image is fleeting for a reason; currents change; tides shift. It's hard to hold onto water.

Elegy for Dracula

Dracula. A contradiction wrapped up in a bat's wing. Evil, charming, deadly, magnetic, brutal, beguiling. The character that Bram Stoker unleashed on the world in 1897 has risen again and again—always in a new form—in stories, in films, in the popular imagination. We think we know him. We don't.

It was summer. We were in high school. The book *Dracula* lay dormant on the shelves of my English department storage room, unread by me.

But the boy I met was charming, magnetic, beguiling, from a different town, a different school. He wore dark madras shorts and a black turtleneck and small, round, dark-framed glasses. I was intrigued by this tall thin figure half in black. And he was intrigued by me. I wish I could remember what I was thinking on the train ride that late-summer day when we had our first date. Or the exact feeling behind our perfect kiss under a tree in the park at the center of town. I only remember calling it perfect in my mind and that no other first kiss has quite matched it.

But then—too soon—he left for boarding school. He sent bulky packages full of black-and-white photographs that he had developed in his school darkroom, and I sent scraps of poetry copied from anthologies stolen from my English department's lounge. We saw each other on his visits home and wrote letters when we were apart. And then late one January night the phone rang. I was a hundred miles away, in bed, wrapped up in plum flannel sheets bleached gray by the moonlight. He had called to tell me he had cut himself. There was blood on the floor, but he had found a bandage. What to say?

For Dracula—all the Draculas—blood is life. But it must constantly be sought. From victims willing or otherwise.

He was sent home.

The next time I saw him was on his sunporch. We sat on the same couch where we had lounged watching movies with his little brother. He was in shorts again, even though it was winter, and a coarsely woven argyle sweater. He would not talk to me, and when I tried to talk to him, he hit himself in the face.

I walked out.

Six months later I left for college. I did not hear from him for over a year.

In November, in a movie theater in Ann Arbor, I saw Francis Ford Coppola's *Dracula* and (being eighteen years old, intense, romantic, incredibly naive) fell unabashedly in love with it. The film takes Dracula's line from the book—"I too can love; you yourselves can tell it from the past"—and runs with it all the way back to the Middle Ages. Stoker's Dracula becomes Vlad the Impaler, who is undone when his beloved wife, Elisabeta, throws herself from a high castle window into the river below. When Dracula learns that she is damned for committing suicide, he renounces the church and becomes a vampire. Four hundred years later Dracula discovers that his lawyer's fiancée, Mina Murray, looks exactly like his dead wife, Elisabeta, and Dracula comes to England to claim her.

My second year at Michigan my dark one, my D, came to the Midwest. It was easy to feel claimed, to pick up where we had left off, despite our terrible breakup and the silence that followed. He was the smartest and most passionate person I had ever met, and I was nineteen; I could handle whatever he dished out. We prowled Ann Arbor's cafés and sipped yerba mattes through metal straws. We scrunched up together in my dorm room's twin bed and read Mary

Shelley, Charlotte Brontë, Pierre Choderlos de Laclos, Anne Rice. When we fought—and when we loved—we often bit and scratched. Once, in the middle of the night, he went next door to stop a terrible fight we heard through the walls. More often the fight was our own.

The Mina Murray in the film is smart, dark haired, writerly. She has worried about her fiancé, Jonathan Harker, who has been out of touch ever since traveling to Transylvania to visit a client, but then she is distracted. On the street in London she meets a foreign prince, whom we immediately recognize as Dracula. He needs directions, and she takes him where he wants to go. But once there, he pulls her into a side room with such smoothness they appear to be gliding. In this temporary privacy he whispers to her in his own language, a dark mumbling of harsh consonants and round vowels, which she seems to understand. His teeth come out at the sight of her exposed neck, but he stops just at the brink of biting her. Does his "human" nature overpower his monstrous instincts? Or is it a desire for something more than blood that stops him? This Mina is more than just a physical conquest, more than just blood to be claimed; she is the exact image of his long-dead wife. It is fate that brings them back together—gliding, irresistible fate.

At the end of my junior year I left my Ann Arbor apartment in D's care and spent the summer in New Hampshire. There I met someone like *Dracula's* Quincey Morris—not a Texan but an adventurer with a straightforward intention to do good—and his light flirtation was different enough from my dark one's attractions that I was intrigued. For his own mysterious reasons D refused to write or call me while I was away—what fate was this?—and his silence made it easier to listen to my Quincey's tales of kayaking the Great Lakes or winter camping on Isle Royale. Soon we were taking long walks in the woods, our pinkie fingers joined, not quite admitting to holding hands. Our last night on Lake Winnipesaukee we shared a cot in the camp's infirmary. Two days later, back in Ann Arbor, I broke up with D.

In the film Dracula woos Mina. They drink absinthe together, which seems to bring back memories of her previous life as Elisabeta. But then Mina hears that Jonathan has returned. She abandons Dracula, who in turn abandons his human guise and falls into a vampiric rage.

D's reaction was bad. I spent the night at a friend's. The next day I returned to my apartment to find that he had moved out but had marked all my book spines with a smear of blood. A few weeks later I moved to a one-room apartment on Church Street.

"My sweet prince," Mina says with fleeting regret. "Jonathan must never know of us." She destroys her diary on her way to the convent where she and Jonathan will be married without delay—or confession. The monstrous Dracula takes his revenge by killing Mina's friend Lucy—and turning her into a vampire. Still, Mina feels tied to him.

I still felt tied to D. Only a year earlier, in my small apartment on South University, D and I had agreed to marry if we were still unmarried by thirty (which then seemed a lifetime away). We planned to meet in New York, in the *Water Lilies* room at the Museum of Modern Art on a certain date, halfway between my thirtieth birthday and his. I was still bound to him, still waiting for his call.

In the film Jonathan assembles a group of men to hunt Dracula down. He leaves Mina alone, and Dracula seizes the moment. He creeps into her room in the form of mist and then materializes not by Mina's bed but in it. When she wakes from her sleep, she welcomes him, calling him her "love." And Dracula loves her too. He insists on explaining who he is—"lifeless, soulless, hated and feared. I am the monster that breathing men would kill; I am Dracula"—but she still loves him. He warns her that "to walk with me you must die to your breathing life and be reborn to mine," but Mina insists, "I want to be what you are, see what you see, love what you love." When she starts to drink the blood from his chest, he stops her. "No," he says, "I cannot let this be . . . I love you too much to condemn you." But Mina drinks willingly.

When I first saw this movie, at nineteen, the idea of a dark immortality was immensely attractive. It was easy to see how Mina would prefer Dracula to Jonathan. Keanu Reeves portrays Jonathan as a wooden prig, which makes it all the more understandable—desirable even—for Mina to turn away from him.

In the movie Dracula has the seductive powers of a confident man as well as the supernatural powers of an immortal. And his control over Mina is intensified by predestination. Mina appears to be Dracula's wife reincarnated, and with the help of Dracula's relentless pursuit, she falls passionately in love with him (again). If I were swept away by Dracula, it wouldn't be my fault. I would be acting under forces beyond my control. I wouldn't leave Jonathan Harker—whoever he was in my life at the time. I would be taken from him. I would be fated to answer his call.

D called when I was in graduate school—long after my Quincey and I had parted ways. Once I flew out to a lonely midwestern town to spend a weekend with him. It happened to be Valentine's Day, and in a gesture of irony we went to Hooters. Once, a year later, we met at a New York café, and on a street corner in Soho he picked me up, twirled me around, and kissed me even though we both belonged to someone else. We always called these "moments out of time." It seemed that in some way we would always be there for each other, that our bond was stronger than that of others, that we could take from each other what we needed—or wanted—regardless of others in our lives. We were each other's future.

Mina appears to be Dracula's future as well as his past. When she drinks his blood, her transformation into a vampire begins. Her husband tries to keep her safe, but she is under the influence of forces greater than all of them. The group of men takes Mina with them as they hunt Dracula across Europe to his castle's very doorstep. There, in a dramatic showdown, he is nearly killed. Mina, still under his spell, drags him inside to safety. And Jonathan, her husband, lets her go.

Then, when I was twenty-nine, I met J.

Within months I knew that he was the one I wanted to spend the rest of my life with. D and I had drifted; we hadn't talked in months, if not years, and I only thought of him after I turned thirty and the day of our meeting approached. But by then I had learned that the Museum of Modern Art had moved to Queens for renovation. And Monet's *Water Lilies* were not in Manhattan or in their temporary home: they were packed up and in transit somewhere in between. I took this as more than a sign.

D and I didn't meet. J proposed during a spring snowstorm in the Bishop's Garden of the National Cathedral, and I said yes. Later that month I started rereading *Dracula*.

The Jonathan in the book is very different from the Jonathan in the movie. In the book he is described as "uncommonly clever . . . [and] also a man of great nerve." His appearance, though, is deceiving. One of the men who helps hunt down Dracula writes, "I was prepared to meet a good specimen of manhood, but hardly the quiet, business-like gentleman who came here today."

When I first met J, he, too, seemed the right content in the wrong form. Instead of the particular "specimen of manhood" I expected, J is my height, slightly built, more of an artist than a scholar, with green eyes and light-brown hair—not the tall, dark stereotype I thought I was holding out for. Just after we met, I left for a two-month teaching job in New England, and our relationship began with a postcard, then a series of letters.

In the book Mina is not distracted by a foreign prince. She suffers in Jonathan's long absence. The reader knows—as Mina does not—that

Jonathan has been kept a prisoner in Dracula's castle. With little outlet for her fears, Mina confines them to her diary. Later she compiles all kinds of documents, including this diary and the other characters' private writing (Jonathan's account of his time in Dracula's castle; a doctor's notes about his patient Lucy; telegrams from the doctor's mentor, Van Helsing; letters between Mina and Lucy) so that they can read their larger story, instead of being limited to their own particular part of it. These documents play a crucial role in their understanding and ultimate defeat of Dracula. Their words save them all—when they have the right reader. Mina is that reader.

When I read *Dracula* in the months after my engagement, I was amazed to see how different Stoker's original story is from Coppola's movie. Stoker's Dracula may be charming but only on the surface. Underneath is a reptilian coldness and inhuman cruelty. He is not a romantic but a predator, not a lover but a monster. His motives are only blood, safety, and survival.

In the book Mina becomes Dracula's greatest victim. With Jonathan asleep beside her, Dracula slips into their bedroom, forcing her to drink his blood. "You," he says, "their best beloved one, are now to me, flesh of my flesh; blood of my blood; kin of my kin; . . . and shall be later on my companion and my helper . . . When my brain says 'Come!' to you, you shall cross land or sea to do my bidding." This is not gliding, resistless fate. This is violent, deliberate, dispassionate evil.

And passion, I think, is the key. We think of *passion* as being romantic or sexual, but its earliest usage refers to the agonies of Christ or a Christian martyr: "senses relating to physical suffering and pain." The word evolved to include both positive and negative feelings: "any strong, controlling, or overpowering emotion, as desire, hate, fear, etc.," and this is what Dracula's victims feel for him. They are all overpowered by him.

Only after the sixteenth century does passion become associated with love, romance, and desire; it becomes the word that we are familiar with. But the third definition of *passion* may surprise us: "Senses relating to passivity . . . The fact or condition of being acted upon; subjection to external force; *esp.* . . . . passivity (opposed to *action*)."

Passion and *passive* share the same root, and it can be easy to confuse them.

I confused them. Time after time I gave up action and responsibility for passionate passivity, gliding, resistless, into what I thought was fate.

In the book, after Dracula has forced Mina to drink his blood and her transformation begins, Jonathan writes in his diary, "To one thing I have made up my mind; if we find out that Mina must be a vampire in the end, then she shall not go into that unknown and terrible land alone." Would Jonathan yield to Mina's vampire call? Would he accompany her to the land of the undead? This would go against everything he believes as a man and as a Christian, and yet it looks as if he would. His willingness shows what kind of man Jonathan really is; he is anything but the uptight prude that Keanu Reeves portrays him as. In fact, he is more of a man than Dracula. He would give not only his life for Mina but also his death—the kind of sacrifice that no other character is willing to make.

But I didn't see any of this until now, now that I have met the man I am going to marry. Before this, Dracula seemed like a dark savior poised to pull me out of whatever bland romance I might be trapped in, and I thought of D in much the same way. Now, though, when I reread the book, I feel Mina's horror when the men burst into her bedroom and pull her bloody mouth from Dracula's breast. I feel the tremors that course through her body as she screams, "Unclean, unclean!" and the guilt that sears her conscience when her husband's hair turns white from shock.

Now, when I watch the movie, I find myself counting the days of Mina and Dracula's happiness against the years of Dracula's loneliness. Mina and Dracula spend only two evenings together—one season perhaps—against more than four centuries of his despair. Now I am less intrigued by Dracula's dark power than I am moved by Jonathan's secret resolution to go with Mina into the darkness, if she is so called, because they wed for life, for better and worse, in sickness and health, and in this case not even un-death would keep them apart.

In the book he doesn't have to follow her into darkness. Dracula is defeated, and Mina is freed from his call, restored to both herself and her husband.

The movie has a different ending—and a different legacy. Its chase also ends at Dracula's castle, where Mina levels a rifle at her own husband. "When my time comes, will you do the same for me?" she asks. In the book Mina wishes to be killed before she fully transforms into a vampire, but the movie's Mina seems to be asking something different. Faced with the challenge in her voice and the barrel of her gun, Jonathan says no. When one of the men rushes at her with a sword, Jonathan stops him. "No," he says, "let them go. Our work is finished here; hers has just begun." Perhaps there is more to this Jonathan than the film gives him credit for, but this is his last line, and there is little to explain it.

Mina and the wounded Dracula retreat to a chapel in his castle, where he dies under the centuries-old painting of his younger self reaching out in a swirl of cape to catch the falling Elisabeta. After centuries apart through death and damnation, they are finally reunited. It reminded me of my plans with D to be buried side by side, to have a tube connect our coffins "to continue our conversation" in the afterlife, and to marry at thirty, to steal whatever "moments out of time" we wanted until then, to keep that call between us. However doomed it was, our love, our passion, was that strong.

When the book's Mina looks back at those months of trial, I imagine she will feel only gratitude that Dracula was defeated and that she has been restored. But I wonder what the movie's Mina thinks after Dracula's death, after the final resolving chords of the soundtrack, after the screen goes black and the credits roll, after she gathers herself and steps outside the castle gates, where her husband, Jonathan, awaits her. What then?

I know that I will marry J. But I also know that I will sometimes be haunted by the fleeting shadow of a figure in black, a glimpse of turtleneck, a drop of blood, the silence that comes before the call, reminders that I have lost something I once cherished, something I can never have again, something I will always carry with me, whether I want it or not.

Ambush

His email was casual enough, but no one sends a note to an ex-girlfriend on Valentine's Day unless he's dissatisfied with his current relationship.

> hpy vday.
> how goes it?
> we're in our thirties, woman.
> isn't it about time for you to not invite me to a wedding?

I had always carried him in the back pocket of my heart. He was my safety net. During my catastrophic breakups, he was always faintly in the background, ready to be called if needed. And he felt the same way about me. At nineteen we decided that if we weren't married to anyone else by thirty, we would marry each other. But by our late twenties we had broken up, gotten back together, broken up again. Thirty came and went in silence. I had thought he was the love of my life.

Yet even when we were faithful to each other, our love had the quality of an affair, and there was always an element of warfare to our relationship. We fancied ourselves something out of *Dangerous Liaisons*—sparring equals to each other but above everyone else. We were as bored by our high school lives as the Marquise de Merteuil and the Vicomte de Valmont were by the high society of the Ancien Régime.

In college, free from our parents and high school, we lost our tempers and withheld ourselves from each other through sulks and long walks and unanswered phone calls. Distrustful, we rifled through desks and hacked into email accounts. We had light flings with others—barely anything more than talk, but to us talk was the deepest form of betrayal. We were like Merteuil and Valmont in that a chevalier might be in my bed and a fiancée in his, but there was still a loyalty, and a love, between us that no other relationship could possibly touch.

This volatile fuel propelled us into our midtwenties, but after that, and after what turned out to be our last breakup, even witty banter seemed difficult. The two hundred miles between our home cities became a no-man's-land, not the challenge it would have been even five years earlier. But still, he was always on the borders of my mind, even when I knew he was living with someone else, even when I was living with someone else.

But then I met J, and my heart emptied its pockets. I left my safety net behind and went AWOL. I married without even telling him I was engaged.

I didn't tell him because by then we had drifted apart. As I far as I knew, he was living with a woman in Brooklyn. But I also didn't tell him because I didn't want him to crash the wedding. At nineteen he had told me that if I married anyone else, he would kneel in the back pew and weep. I didn't want even a scrap of worry that this might happen on my wedding day. So I didn't tell him, and it didn't happen.

But then, nearly two months later, I got his Valentine's Day email: "isn't it about time for you to not invite me to a wedding?"

I could imagine what it would have felt like if he had been the one to marry first, if my safety net were whisked away and spread under someone else, that feeling of being exposed on the trapeze and knowing, as I reached for the next pair of outstretched hands, that there was nothing below to catch me.

Alone at my computer, I stared at his email, hands in my lap, keyboard silent, eyes dry, wondering what to say. Outside a truck passed, its motor churning up Connecticut Avenue.

I waited three days, and then I spent at least thirty minutes crafting these few lines:

"My thirties are treating me awfully well so far—and not quite two months ago, actually, I didn't invite you to my wedding. He's not the ex-academic foreign-car-mechanic you predicted for me, but close—he repairs and restores violins and bows. It feels odd to tell you this via email—but I hope this news finds you well. What are you up to these days?"

I hated the words I wrote, the light tone and chatty details that seemed like tinsel over a bomb. But what more could I say? The less the better, I thought. His email to me had felt like an ambush, my past leaping from the bushes into the straight path I was trying to cut through the forest. I didn't want to confront it, but there it was, uncoiled and sprung straight at my heart.

He didn't wait three days to write back. Later that afternoon he replied that somehow he had almost already known. He said he was happy for me—and nauseated. He said he felt a mix of congenial pride slowly crowding out the urge to "rend my clothes and claw at my eyeballs."

This I expected. When I had thought about how I would feel if our situations were reversed, I imagined something akin to rending and clawing. I could imagine another Valentine's Day slipping by, lonely and alone or worse: lonely with someone else, drinking coffee with him in the morning, eating steak across a table from him in the evening and lying beside him at night, staring at the ceiling, hoping he was already asleep, wishing for sleep to come so the day would finally be over. That's the worst kind of loneliness.

And then, three days later, to find the love of your life married to someone else, your safety net transformed into a snare that has trapped you with your worst fear. Your expected liaison has turned into an ambush, and now you have to return to that empty apartment or to that table, that bed, that someone beside you. This would be nearly unbearable.

He said he was living with someone: "We're at a turning point, but I have hope."

I'm embarrassed to admit that when I first read that phrase, I thought he meant we were at a turning point, he and I, not he and his someone. That's how unwilling I was even then to let go of our fantasy—the trust that we would always be there for each other—even when I had married away from this expectation, this security, this hope.

He went on: "i have a fire escape with a greenhouse, a cat, a red couch, a brisket in a crockpot timed to finish at five, and you . . . you have my best wishes."

How much did he think about that comma? His use of the word *and*? Did he think he still had me? Or did he just want to remind me of my old feelings, to rekindle them, to keep me in the game? And did part of me still want to play?

I wrote back:

I'm glad you wrote what you wrote. It was hard to figure out how to tell you, since I had wondered quite a bit throughout the years how I would feel if it was you telling me. Right now I'd be crazy happy for you, but three years ago it would have been my rent clothes and clawed eyeballs. I'm glad your reaction isn't entirely rent and clawed.

I hope those four years have been good ones. I have no fire escape, no greenhouse (just windowsills), no cat, a suede-y brown couch, no brisket, a pile of chocolate chip cookies in Tupperware, a multiyear contract at the 85th "top" university, and now a husband (which still sounds funny to my ear), but still the same best wishes for you.

I thought a lot about the last sentence of his email and how mine could answer it and where to put the comma. I consciously used a *but* instead of an *and*—the conjunction that doesn't join two things together but turns from one to another. Part of me wanted to let him know that what we once had was irrevocably over. Part of me wanted to let him know how hard it was to end this fantasy. But I couldn't then admit to myself that I wanted it both ways.

I didn't write again. I allowed myself to feel relieved at his response, but I didn't believe he was letting me have anything: not relief, not closure and not his best wishes.

And I was right.

A year later he wrote again. He was moving from the East Coast to a big straight-bordered state in the middle of the country. He said he had been more upset than he had let on: "it was every bit as awful as i wasn't able to imagine. just . . . bad. typed off the congratulation and took a solemn oath not to say another word for a full calendar year. consider it a wedding present."

I felt the same twist in my stomach as when I imagined him kneeling and weeping in the back pew. In high school we had been enemies and allies. He had stalked me in college, but I was a willing victim. Later, when we lived in cities separated by two hundred miles of interstate, our phone calls and emails had a tricky, sly, testing quality to them, and I wondered what lay beneath our carefully orchestrated conversations. What scheme? What kind of game? And now, what had lain dormant beneath our silence?

After the Marquise de Merteuil and the Vicomte de Valmont have exchanged letters throughout *Dangerous Liaisons*, letters that have charted their plans to seduce women and ruin men, to rekindle their affair or declare themselves enemies, Valmont loses patience with the woman. "As of today," he writes, "I shall be your lover or your enemy." The decision is hers—"A couple of words will do."

Merteuil responds with four: "Very well; it's war!" From this exchange a series of betrayals leads to Valmont's death and Merteuil's exile.

Instead of provoking or proclaiming a declaration of war, I sent a carefully constructed email wishing him some Kerouac-y adventures on his trip west, which, to my enduring ambivalence, prompted no response at all.

II

Shadows and Markings

The Shadow of the Hours

New York, 2000.

I first read *The Hours* when I had all the hours in the world.

The Hours: London, England, 1923.

Virginia Woolf awakens from a dream of cream-colored roses to find herself in her bedroom at Hogarth House. She rises, avoids the mirror as she washes her face, pours a cup of coffee, and goes downstairs to her husband. There "she stands tall, haggard, marvelous in her housecoat, the coffee steaming in her hand. He is still, at times, astonished by her . . . Her books may be read for centuries. He believes this more ardently than does anyone else. And she is his wife." She has no way of acknowledging his unspoken admiration. She goes upstairs to write. Here, in her own room, "there are infinite possibilities, whole hours ahead . . . She may pick up her pen and follow it with her hand as it moves across the paper; she may pick up her pen and find that she's merely herself, a woman in a housecoat holding a pen . . . She picks up her pen. *Mrs. Dalloway said she would buy the flowers herself.*"

The Hours: Los Angeles, 1949.

Laura Brown is still in bed, reading the first lines of *Mrs. Dalloway*: "Mrs. Dalloway said she would buy the flowers herself." When she gets to the lark, the plunge, this moment in June, she throws the covers back on her own June morning, pulls on a robe, and pads downstairs, hesitating for a moment before joining her husband. He has already made coffee. There are a dozen white roses on the table. When she enters, he is "delighted." But when she pours a cup of coffee and kisses his cheek, he "pats her rump affectionately and absentmindedly. He is no longer thinking of her. He is thinking about the day ahead of him." Later he will praise the cake she has baked with no knowledge of the day she has had, the ruined first cake, her retreat to a hotel room to read, her brush with suicide, her secret wish to hold a "touch of brilliance herself, just a hint of it"—the genius Virginia Woolf had in abundance and that Leonard Woolf recognized in silence. Dan Brown does not know his wife at all.

Washington DC, 2003.

A dark November night. A woman is deep into writing an essay called "Fracturing *The Hours*," which is meant to propel her into a doctoral program, to save her from a dead-end teaching job, to change her life. She hasn't written a scholarly essay in years, but she is determined to say something about these two works. But in her mind it is so much more brilliant than what appears on the page. She tries to apply literary theories that she doesn't fully understand. She tries to follow a friend's advice—a friend who already has a PhD—to make it "sexy." She tries, but instead she writes passages of elaborate summary, with quotes from Woolf and Cunningham featured like gemstones in the plain metal setting of her words. She does what she tells her students not to do. She leans on others' ideas because she has so few of her own. She fears that she is becoming Laura Brown, wishing for genius but baking a crooked cake instead.

Washington DC, 2003.

A bright November morning. The woman in her kitchen, wearing her boyfriend's robe, a cup of coffee he has just brewed hot in her hand, a vase of white roses on the table behind him. J knows she is frightened at how inadequate "Fracturing *The Hours*" is. He says, "I know you can do this." And suddenly she know that he thinks she can, that he thinks she is something close to genius and that although she is not yet his wife, she is still his. It is surreal. All the details of the scenes she has been reading suddenly sharpen into focus: she is wearing the same robe as Virginia Woolf and Laura Brown; she is drinking the same coffee; her Leonard in the form of J thinks she's marvelous; her Dan—also in the form of J—doesn't yet entirely understand who she is or what she's trying to achieve; the same white roses haunt the background, a total coincidence.

In *The Hours* Virginia Woolf writes *Mrs. Dalloway*, Laura Brown reads it, and Clarissa Vaughn lives a modern American version of it. But now the story has come loose from its moorings. Here in my own kitchen I become the fourth woman in *The Hours*. Just as Virginia Woolf didn't imagine Laura Brown reading *Mrs. Dalloway*, Cunningham never imagined me reading *The Hours*. But here I am, living out yet another storyline—tacking like a sailboat between others' lives.

I have often intensely wanted to marry someone completely unsuitable for me—someone with whom marriage would be, in effect, emotional suicide. Maybe I just wanted the decision to be over. I wanted to commit, even if it was to the wrong thing, just to have the question answered, to stop wondering, speculating, guessing—to live in the present, unhaunted by "if."

Virginia Stephen's marriage to Leonard Woolf looked at first as unlikely a match. She was high-strung, patrician, and uncertain about sex; he was poor, Jewish, and desirous. She treated their engagement like a joke: their announcement to mutual friend Lytton Strachey was signed:

Ha! Ha!
Virginia Stephen
Leonard Woolf.

On her honeymoon she would read *Crime and Punishment* and *Le Rouge et le noir*. A year earlier, as Leonard was returning from Ceylon, she read *Les Liaisons dangereuses*. I wonder what Virginia was reading during her weeks of deliberation, just before she took the plunge that would alter the course of her life forever and, ten years into her marriage, lead her to write: "The immense success of our life, is I think, that our treasure is hid away; or rather in such common things that nothing can touch it . . . sitting down after dinner, side by side, & saying 'Are you in your stall, brother?'—well, what can trouble this happiness? And every day is necessarily full of it."

And then, in the last hours of her life, a suicide note: "I don't think two people could have been happier than we have been."

I wrote the essay and mailed out my graduate school applications in the darkest days of winter, and during the three cold months of waiting, I thought back to the fall before, when J and I drove through the dark woods of West Virginia and plotted our future. I remembered when we found a letterpress stationery store and how our eyes met over the section of wedding invitations.

In March the mailbox finally delivered what I didn't know I had been waiting for. With each thin envelope, each rejection, I felt another wave of relief, and the very last made me smile when I read its "We regret . . ." There. The choice I had been slowly making was sealed. I would not throw myself into an academic program; I would take a different plunge. I would write. And I would stay with J.

Reader, I married him. I did not read *The Hours* again for a long time. I did not want to feel its shadow or be pulled by its conflicting gravity.

Washington DC, 2010.

Another dark winter. I sit in a chair in my living room, my world shrunk to arm's reach. I am pregnant with twins, and as the days shorten and my belly grows, the weight of what I am carrying presses me down and down, deeper and deeper into stagnation and depression. Perhaps I could have managed one—but not two. I fear that they will eat me up. I fear that my life is already over, the remaining months of pregnancy merely a stay.

I sit in the chair next to a bookcase. In that bookcase is *The Hours*.

I will not read it. I turn its spine to face away. I remember all too well Laura Brown's efforts to avoid the searching eyes of her son, the bland but insistent affection of her husband, her flight to a hotel room, the image of that water surging up to cover and claim her. I remember her vowing, "I will want this second child"—the child she is carrying as she reads *Mrs. Dalloway*, as she desperately tries to hew out space for herself in her claustrophobic life, the child that will bind her to that life all the more tightly. But I will not read it. I will not think about it. I will want this second child.

Leaving the Island

Halfway through *Robinson Crusoe*, Crusoe finds a human footprint in the sand. He is terrified. After fifteen years alone on his desert island, the thought of another person drives him nearly mad with fear.

I did not see a footprint. I saw a sonogram. But it was not just a single image. I was carrying twins.

My husband and I have no history of twins in our families. We had no help conceiving them. That particular month my ovaries, perhaps feeling the pinch of time, decided to fire off both barrels, sending out two eggs instead of one, two eggs to be fertilized, two eggs to implant, two eggs to hatch into two new human beings, twice as much genetic material to fling against eternity.

I pretended to be shocked into silence when the sonogram reader said, "It's twins!" and my husband smiled through his happy tears and pressed my hand. I pretended to be merely stunned when the nurse took my blood ("I'm a twin!" she told me brightly). I pretended to be simply overwhelmed as I filled out forms and made our next appointment and kept my eyes slightly wide and my mouth pulled into what I hoped looked like a bemused smile. But I, like Crusoe, was "terrified to the last degree."

When I stepped into the elevator, I entered what would become my nine-month Island of Despair. I put on my sunglasses and cried. I cried in the elevator, in the lobby, on the walk to the car, in the car, on the drive home, and then flung across my bed. I cried through the afternoon and evening and sporadically through the night. When I woke up—eyes swollen, nose blocked, heart dark and dry—I felt nothing but despair at the wreck I thought my life had become.

In the morning after his wreck, Crusoe is comforted by the sight of his ship driven nearly to shore, and he spends the first day salvaging what he can from it. But I could not see a way forward with twins. I was convinced that I would be completely consumed by them, that I would be unable to have any kind of independent life, that I would have to somehow hold myself in suspended animation until they turned eighteen, when maybe, just maybe, I might be able to recover some of the things that made me me. While everyone else was thrilled by the news, I felt myself sinking further and further into hermetic misery.

Robinson Crusoe is a novel that explores what it is to be an individual in isolation. Crusoe is cast off from human company and stranded for nearly three decades on his South Pacific island, which the locals call Masafuera, which means "Farther Away." During the first few years he goes through cycles of grief and resignation, faith and despair, hope and fear. But all this time he is making practical improvements to his island—a fortress, a garden, flocks, furniture. And that is part of what makes this book so compelling. We can't help but ask ourselves what we would do in his place. What home would we build for ourselves? What books would we wish we had? What fantasies and philosophies would we spin out into the barren days and silent nights?

But depression is a different kind of island. It is also isolated, but its resources are inaccessible. Depression is a place no one can really fathom until or unless he is there. It is a place where logic fails. It is a place where the laws of gravity are more powerful than any other force. It is a place almost impossible to revisit or describe once you've left.

That fall my island was my living room, my fortress an Ikea Poang chair. I did not make practical improvements to my environment other than the most basic preparations for the twins: two rocking cradles, a changing table, diapers, blankets, onesies (a word I didn't even know how to pronounce pre-pregnancy—*oh-ness-ies*?). I tried to work on an essay or at least write some journal entries, but I couldn't seem to make sentences form. I tried to read some of my favorite books—*Anna*

Karenina, The Hobbit—but after staring, unseeing, at their pages for many minutes, I burned through all the Sookie Stackhouse novels on my Kindle, ordering the next only minutes after finishing the last. When reading became too difficult, I tried to watch movies like *The Life Aquatic with Steve Zissou* and the new Sherlock Holmes on PBS, but then I realized I couldn't follow a simple plot let alone an intellectual mystery, so I streamed series like *Firefly* and *The Hills*, clicking WATCH NEXT over and over and over again. I could barely believe how stupid I felt, but I would do anything to distract myself from my fears of being cannibalized and colonized from the inside out. It turns out there was some truth to these fears.

Later I read that a woman's brain can shrink by 8 percent over the course of her pregnancy. The fetus siphons off all her juicy omega-3 fatty acids and other brain-plumping nutrients, and her brain downsizes to compensate. I have become convinced that, because I was carrying twins, my brain shrank 16 percent.

And then I read that cells from a fetus can migrate through the placenta and take up residence in the mother's body. A mother's brain might contain her child's cells. A child's cells could indeed colonize her mother's brain.

This condition is called "chimerism," named after the mythological Chimera that Homer describes in the *Iliad* as "a thing of immortal make, not human, lion-fronted and snake behind, a goat in the middle, and snorting out the breath of the terrible flame of bright fire." In Greek myth a sighting of the Chimera might portend storms and shipwrecks, but Crusoe never saw one. He has little warning of the violent hurricane that drives his ship off course and into his small island.

The footprint, however, warns of a different danger. Lying awake night after night, he is at first convinced that the footprint is the Devil's and then tries to convince himself that it is actually his own footprint. But he finally concludes that the print belongs to one of "the savages of the mainland," a cannibal. Crusoe spends the next few years camouflaging his living quarters and securing his livestock and making his presence on the island as invisible as possible.

But there is no hiding a twin pregnancy. Around my fifth month people started asking me when I was due. "Mamma's gonna pop!" a man yelled at me on the street. But by my third trimester I wasn't going out much anymore. My waist had reached Henry VIII proportions. I had outgrown my maternity clothes and took to wearing a tank top and two receiving blankets pinned together to make a loincloth. My physical self kept growing as my internal self was slowly eaten away.

After fantasizing all kinds of fears, Crusoe finally sees evidence of the "savage wretches" who use his island's beaches as a feasting ground, leaving behind "skulls, hands, feet, and other bones of human bodies." He muses, "Fear of danger is ten thousand times more terrifying than danger itself," and then spends quite some time planning ways to eradicate this "evil" by killing the cannibals through elaborate plots involving pits full of gunpowder. But then he has a dream. Crusoe rescues one of the cannibals and civilizes him, and in gratitude the former savage shares his knowledge of the sea, allowing Crusoe to escape the island.

And that, of course, is exactly what happens. The rescued Friday becomes his "servant, and, perhaps, a companion or assistant," and the two become inseparable, leaving the island and, after many adventures, returning to England together.

I did not have a dream to show me the way forward. In fact, I was barely sleeping. My days were a fog of crushing weight, itchy skin, swollen feet, and endless thirst, my nights a darker and lonelier version of the same. I was in no shape to rescue anyone, least of all myself. I gave in to the island and waited.

At four o'clock in the morning on the day the twins were born, I heard the first birds of spring singing outside my window. My hands were shaking so badly I could barely sign the hospital admittance forms, but my mind was a smooth sheet of calm sea. When I delivered the twins, my body was not wrecked but carefully cut open and even more carefully repaired. I was not cannibalized or colonized, and when the twins left my body, my terrible despair did too. Perhaps it was the relief at being sole again. Perhaps it was the ebb of a hormonal flood. But that first night, as the twins slept in their hospital cribs, I turned to my husband and said, "Don't tell anyone, but they're pretty cool."

I was delivered too.

Behind the Caves

Only connect.

E. M. Forster

At my twenty-year high school reunion I learned that the most popu-lar girl in school—the Queen—had married one of the Hoods. How had this happened?

Everything felt mysterious. I had just had twins. My body did not feel like my own. I was incredibly tired and morbidly sensitive, and my mind felt dilated—like an aperture—the film behind it overex-posed and unable to process.

On the tour of our school I deliberately hung back, the last to enter a room and the last to leave. Here was the front desk where you signed in if you were late. Here was the hall lined with class pictures, including one with a famous actress camouflaged amid the smooth, blurred faces. Here was the auditorium where I played Corelli concertos and *Hello, Dolly!* on my violin. Only now the auditorium was condemned. We stood just inside its doors, lights off, straining to see the stage, the scent of wood and dust and warm velvet and an intangible nostalgia flooding me like a dark tide.

At the reunion I took stock of who had come. Not my friend the Brain. Not my friend the Hippie. Not my on-again, off-again Crush. Not my stand partner and Rival. No one from my AP English class. No one from my bus route. Not the Queen of the school. Not the Outcast either.

I knew the Outcast the way everyone in a class of one hundred knows each other. But we had never crossed paths, never spoken, until our senior year. Once, just before a concert, I was ripping through a bunch of Vivaldi arpeggios to warm up. I went faster and faster, just to the edge of lost control, and then bent a four-note double-stop to finish. I had thought I was alone, but he had been behind me. "Wow," he said. I tossed my hair over my shoulder and looked at him.

The Queen was not at the reunion, but her Handmaidens were. They looked almost the same—impeccable clothes, perfect hair, still together. They smiled and hugged me, but I was shy, unable to forget, even after twenty years, their little kitten teeth and pin-sharp claws, their bites and barbs. Did they remember?

I wanted to ask them what their life was like then. Did they go to clubs in the city? Did they have midnight pool parties? Either then or now, I couldn't imagine how they, the Coolest of the Cool, had lived.

I didn't go to parties, didn't have a pool, went to the city but never to clubs. The Brain and I played in our state's youth symphony. We wrote poems and staged fake fistfights in a field by a busy road. We talked—a lot—in the woods behind my house, on the deck behind hers, in my gray station wagon, in her little yellow pickup truck.

The Hippie and I ate pizza and made mixtapes. We drew phallic symbols on phone booths with red nail polish and tried to light them on fire. We read Shakespeare over the phone and shopped for Chinese slippers and dangly earrings at Pier 1. We talked—a lot—in her cloud-painted room in the little house across the railroad tracks.

The Outcast wore a trench coat in the spring, in summer bucks without socks, in winter a Snowy River hat. He drove a dark Buick with impressive fins, if you were impressed by that sort of thing. His handwriting was cramped and slanted, and he favored sepia-toned sheets torn carefully from a legal pad. When did he start passing notes to me? And what did the notes say?

After high school one friend got married. One stayed home. One fled north. I went west.

My parents still live in the house I grew up in. When I go back for visits, I drive by the school, sometimes walk around the track, sometimes sit in the bleachers, remembering, wondering. This is where we had a lunchtime picnic of crepes filled with Reddi-wip. This is where the boys called us "dykes," and I wasn't entirely sure what they meant. This is where the smoking lounge used to be. This is where I missed the bus. This is where I missed the point.

With the letters there was a tape. The first song, and the theme of it, was Tom Petty's "I Won't Back Down." Why had he given me this? What had I needed to face, what ground did I need to stand, what easy way out was refused? I don't remember. I don't remember the conversations we had or what I might have confided in him. But it had been important enough for him to record an hour and a half of Memorex tape, music to soothe and bolster me, music to hold me up not at school but at home, in the privacy of my room at night, a place he never saw, an entrance he was never allowed.

At the reunion I was amazed to see a network of relationships—some formed in high school, some after—that I had never known about. People I thought had been good friends were actually better friends with someone else. That's when I started to doubt my own history, my own story.

I wound up talking with people I had barely spoken with in high school. At thirty-eight we were mostly doing the same things: working, raising families. It was easy to find common ground. It was less easy to get at the truth.

The Outcast and I ended almost as soon as we began. At school we were circumspect, but in the afternoons I went to his house. His mother made me Twinings Yunnan tea, smoky and strong, a tea I have not been able to find since. And then she went upstairs, and we went to the basement.

There was a pool table. Did we play? Did we talk? He kissed me, I know, and I kissed him back. But when he boosted me up on the table and wrapped my legs around his waist, I froze.

"What are you doing?" I asked.

"I'm going to make love to you," he said.

The Football Player couldn't believe I wasn't on Facebook. The Football Player and I had never spoken before, but somehow here we were, me recognizing him, him having little idea who I was then ("You played flute, right?") or now. I tried to explain the value I place on privacy, but finally I just laughed a little and said that I'd get on it, but I'd probably choose the anonymous icon instead of posting pictures of myself. "See—some things never change!" he said. I kept my smile in place but looked away. Who was I to these people? Not the Writer. Not the Violinist. I was Not Anyone at All.

On the pool table I said, "Uh, no you're not," in a voice that wasn't my own but borrowed from Claire Standish, Brenda Walsh, or *Some Kind of Wonderful*. I broke his hold and left. I don't remember saying anything else as I walked out, or in school the next day, or when he called or when he wrote. I remember holding my silence up as a wall to keep out . . . what?

Virginia Woolf once wrote (of the draft that would become *Mrs. Dalloway*): "I dig out beautiful caves behind my characters . . . The idea is that the caves shall connect, & each comes to daylight at the present moment."

After the reunion Facebook revealed connections I had never imagined. When had this happened? Immediately after Facebook took off, in 2006 or 2007, when we were all in our midthirties and trying to settle into our adult lives—or escape from them? The ten-year reunion would have already passed ("All the hookups that didn't happen in high school happened then," the Class Secretary told me drily), but there were at least five years to fill before the twenty-year reunion. Some connections, some relationships, some longings, were, I'm sure, ripe for rekindling.

After I looked up the Brain and the Hippie and my Crush and my Rival, I looked up the Outcast. Like Mark Zuckerberg in the last scene of *The Social Network*, I had been tempted to use a friend request as an apology. I looked at his profile picture. He was still handsome, with a boyish curl to his hair—what had made him an outcast? I looked at his friends—plenty of them. And then, among them, I saw the Redhead.

I hadn't known they were friends—on Facebook, in real life, or in high school. But her presence there made me pause. I had barely known him. I had no idea what kind of life he led in the countless hours I wasn't in it. Maybe the Outcast wasn't an outcast. Maybe I had been the Outcast all along.

The web of connections I found on Facebook became more like a fence to me. I was outside and uncertain how much I wanted to be in.

Still, I made a few tentative overtures to other Quiet Girls and was stunned by how different our perceptions of high school were. One thought the Coolest of the Cool were the Sports, not the Preps. One categorized me as part of the Nerd Elite. More and more I felt my own story slipping away from me as other memories challenged my own.

Immediately after the reunion, I had burned to be frozen in people's minds at the age of seventeen—skinny, long-haired, bookish, on the edges, at the margins, holed up in my adolescent introversion, known only by a few who have since become lost to me.

But now the burn of frustration has shifted into a burn of near-shame: how had I not realized that everyone else had been frozen in my mind too? While I thought everyone was dozing along with me in the enchanted castle, they were meeting and talking, going out and hooking up, rekindling old friendships, making new marriages, babysitting each other's children, and posting pictures of all of this on Facebook.

I did not care to dig beyond my cave, and now it feels too late.

I wish I had responded differently as I was perched on that pool table. "I'm going to make love to you." Maybe it was something he had seen in a movie, and weren't we all, at that age, fumbling our lines?

Maybe all those rebuffs—the few I gave, the many I received—were just ways of protecting ourselves, those nascent beings so unsure of who we were or what we wanted to become. We were just beginning to dig our caves, but were still so desperate, yet so afraid—some of us still—to only connect.

Marked

When I can't sleep at night, my hand strays across my belly and fingers the stretch marks on my side.

One is particularly deep. I poke my fingertip into its crater and wonder what I am touching, what layer of skin or tissue. I consider how it was slowly worn from the incremental and unremitting growth of pregnancy. What relentless power to rend the body, even its skin.

I remember the day I discovered my stretch marks: Christmas 2010. I was seven months pregnant—with twins—and thought I had stretched this far without a ripple. But the bathroom mirror in my parents' house hung lower than my own. I saw below my equator, like looking at the far side of the moon—a place long held secret, now revealed to be pitted and pocked, like a wind-ridged desert.

I sighed. This was not a gift I wanted.

The body that once held two human beings now holds memory. The memory of the undeniably gorgeous body I had at sixteen. Of the Indian summer that same-but-different body had at thirty-six—lithe and stronger than it had ever been after many hours and two ranks of aikido. The memory of the afternoon the twins were conceived and the morning they were born. Of my incredulity at the twins' size, beauty, and immediate, discrete personhood. Of the disbelief that I was finally delivered not only of them but also of the physical burden they placed on me: over fifteen pounds of baby and perhaps another fifteen of their accoutrements. The memory of their constant presence and my inability to ever leave them—even for a moment— not for a stiff drink, a pot of coffee, a winter evening walk, or a full night's sleep. The morning they were born my body was freed, my soul ever more bound.

Well, my body was almost free.

It took days to peel away the glue left from the surgical tape covering my incision. It took weeks for the stitches to dissolve and one appointment to have the last one pulled out with a tiny flash of unexpected pain. It took months for the scar to fade from a wet red and years before it dulled to a thin purple line. The loose skin and map of stretch marks will not go away unless I choose to cut them away. I do not choose to remove these parts of myself because I believe that this is what happens to bodies—they carry and stretch and age and scar. This is an important part of being a human being. I believe that changing my shape through surgery would somehow alter who I am, and I don't want to alter who I am. This is what I look like because this is the way I've lived. I would sooner cut away my fast walk, my peculiar handwriting, my particular singing voice.

Still. Still.

I mourn the body I have lost. But it is like mourning my time as a single woman when I married. Or a childless woman when I became a mother. This kind of mourning is often misunderstood, but it is necessary. I loved my life when I was young and free, the many adventures I had and the mistakes I made, the romances and the irresponsibility and the knowledge that my future was wide open. But then I met my mate and happily traded possibilities for one rich certainty. When we decided to try for a child, we traded our joint possibilities for another certainty: we knew that our lives would never be the same. Our past lives are worth mourning, and mourning them in no way diminishes the life we live now. One person encompasses many lives.

The origin of the word *capacity* comes from the Latin *capere*, "to take or hold." After my body no longer held the twins, its excesses subsided. The fluids I had retained slowly drained away. My ankles reappeared. My uterus returned to the size of a pear. My incision healed. My belly tightened. I drank a lot of coffee and a little bourbon, took long walks, slept lying down instead of propped up, did cobra pose in yoga, zipped but couldn't quite button an old pair of jeans.

Now at night I lie in the dark and feel the marks that stipple my skin. These spots and blemishes, these symbols and signs, these imprints and impacts. They remind me that I have been stretched to capacity—beyond capacity—and then managed to stretch further still. And hold.

III

Biologies

The Heart as a Torn Muscle

Overview

Your heart was already full, but then you saw him and your heart beat code, not Morse but a more insistent pulse: Oh yes. That's him. That one.

Not The One (The One you already have—and deeply love), but of all the people in that large room far from home, he was the one for you. And your heart stretched more than it should have, tore a little, and let him in.

Symptoms

- Swelling, bruising, or redness. The feeling that your lungs contain a higher percentage of oxygen and have somehow grown in their capacity to respire. A heightened sensitivity to glances, postures, gestures, attitudes, and casual remarks from observers. A propensity to blush.
- Pain at rest. General restlessness. An inability to sleep. Fever dreams. Sleepwalking. Conscious walking: out of your bedroom, out of doors, into the moonlight or an unmown field shrouded in mist and ache (or fantasies of same).
- Pain when the specific muscle is used. When your heart beats to force blood through your femoral arteries, to your iliopsoas muscles, your sartorius muscles, your peroneus muscles, each expanding and contracting to force your legs to walk away, from him, from thrill, from all the promise and potential of an alternate future.
- Inability to use the muscle at all. Lethargy. Apathy. Malaise. Especially after having walked away from the one in question.

Self-Care

- Apply ice: cool it. The early application of heat can increase swelling and pain. Note: Ice or heat should not be applied to bare skin. Always use a protective layer—latex only as a very last resort, clothing is better or, better still, several feet, a separate piece of furniture, a wall, or a building. Ideally: a state line, a continent.
- Try an anti-inflammatory such as herbal tea or a pro/con list. Cool showers and brisk walks in bracing air may help. Do not take depressants in the form of alcohol or otherwise. Avoid stimulants: caffeine, chocolate, Cheetos.
- Protect the strained muscle from further injury by refusing to jump into anything. Avoid the activities that caused the strain and other activities that are painful.
- Compression. Hold yourself together.
- Elevation. Rise above.

When to Seek Care

If home remedies bring no relief in twenty-four hours, call your youngest and most bohemian friend.

If you hear a "popping" sound, signifying a break from your primary relationship, the one (The One) you truly know and truly love, call your closest and most trusted friend.

Exams and Tests

Your youngest and most bohemian friend asks,

> Are you going to run away together, tryst in motels, meet
>   up in Paris, open a P.O. box, wear a trench coat, give each
>   other code names, assume another identity?
> Would he be up for a threesome?
> Want to use my place?
> Says, It's so romantic.
> Says, Tell me everything!

Your closest and most trusted friend asks,

What do you mean, "met someone"?
Have you thought this through?
Is this choice supporting, adding to, enriching, complicating,
    marring, degrading, not even leaving a blip on the screen in
    the way in which you will see your life in the years to come?
What will you be left with? Regret? Memory? Or absolutely
    nothing?
Says, Time wounds all heels.
Says, Don't fuck up.

Recommended Reading

Anna Karenina by Leo Tolstoy
The Bridges of Madison County by Robert James Waller
Time Will Darken It by William Maxwell
The Lone Pilgrim by Laurie Colwin
Mrs. Dalloway by Virginia Woolf
"The Littoral Zone" by Andrea Barrett
The End of the Affair by Graham Greene

No horoscopes. No tarot cards or tea leaves. If you must, you may
steep yourself in stories of passion and price. Years from now you can
indulge in what-ifs. But for now, right now, put your hand to your
chest and feel what beats. The only muscle you can't live without
needs to stay whole.

A Pill to Cure Love

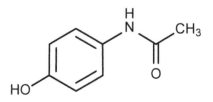

If you Google "a pill to cure love," it will tell you to take Tylenol. But only the recommended dose. Too much, and your liver will malfunction and then your already malfunctioning heart.

Tylenol is a brand name for acetaminophen. *Acetaminophen* is composed of syllables taken from its three chemical components: acetyl, amino, and phenol.

Acetyl

comes from *acetic*, from the Latin *acetum*, "vinegar" (properly *vinum acetum*, "wine turned sour"). Left open for too long, what was once intoxicating turns bleak.

In cooking you can add vinegar to correct for sweetness. In love you can add acetaminophen to correct for its loss.

You can also use vinegar to remove scorch marks and sweat stains from fabrics; to clean glass, banish weeds, and kill germs; to prevent cracked eggs, loosen a rusty screw, and remove dead skin.

These are such practical uses. But all the lover wants is to burn—sweaty, overgrown, whole, screwed tight, bright, and alive.

Amino

forms the root of *ammonia*, a colorless gas with a smell that can snap a reluctant consciousness back into its body with one sharp breath.

Like vinegar, ammonia can clean burn marks on glass, strip tarnish from silver, remove stains from clothing. It can also repel moths, keep them from making holes in your clothes, keep them from the flame that draws and draws and kills.

Ammonia is also used in fertilizers and explosives, in opposites, in contradictions. Because of this, it seems a *pharmakon* in the cure for love.

Phenol

is also known as carbolic acid. It was discovered in coal tar in the early 1800s, and John Lister pioneered its use as an antiseptic in the early 1900s.

Unlike vinegar and ammonia, carbolic acid smells sweet. It is used in perfumes and lubricants, to adorn and ease love. Undiluted, it is poisonous, causes burns, convulsions, stupor.

But under the body's surface, when coupled with amines and acetyl, when it has been absorbed through the digestive system and into the nervous system, acetaminophen can soothe the after-scorch of love.

I take two Tylenol with a large glass of water and think of our dissolution. How I held the sweet shell of you in my mouth, not knowing what bitter chalk lay beneath, not knowing how easily the shell would rupture, how the rancor within would flood and calcify.

But the Tylenol hold their shape past my throat and dissolve in my stomach. They pass through the bloodstream to the liver, where their real work begins.

The liver purifies toxins. It filters out all that the metaphorical heart thinks it can take—too much sugar, too much fat, too much richness. It converts nutrients into substances that the body can use. The liver is a pragmatist. The liver is the antidote to the lover.

In the body prostaglandins transmit pain signals, but here in the liver acetaminophen is absorbed to block them. Return this pain to sender. The number you have dialed is no longer in service. The fever you once induced has been broken. This account has been deactivated.

But as with any spell, the user must be careful. Too much acetaminophen and the liver fails, overwhelmed by the toxins its job is to strain. The cure for love becomes a burden to the heart. The heart fails, the body dies.

But just two Tylenol—taken every four to six hours, for a few days, some white nights, a week, perhaps a month—reduces the fever, dulls the pain, metabolizes the love affair. Vinegar, ammonia, tar. They keep the liver alive and filtering out all that was already lost until the remnants are ready to be released by the body, the lover, the one who once loved.

What of the Raven, What of the Dove?

A story was growing inside my neck, but I didn't yet know what it said.

After the first appointment I started Terry Tempest Williams's *Refuge*. In the weeks between the ultrasound and biopsy, I read about the rise of the Great Salt Lake, the displacement of its birds, the spread of Williams's mother's cancer, her slow relentless death.

I read this while I waited.

The first robins of spring arrived, and I pointed them out to my two-year-old twins. They soon became expert at spotting robins. There was one in the mulch under the bush; there was one on the edge of the sidewalk; there was one in the tree outside their window. They looked back at us almost balefully, like portly English gentlemen in wooly red vests, peering out of the nineteenth century, unsure what to make of our present.

I wonder if Williams, as she identified avocets and counted egrets, knew that the Romans studied birds to determine the will of the gods. That *auspice*, *auger*, and *avian* share a Latin root. Did she seek prophecy in burrowing owls, in snow buntings? Or could she see all too clearly what lay ahead?

What growth to feed ~~and what growth to excise~~ is a matter of perspective.

"Erasure," Williams writes in *When Women Were Birds: Fifty-Four Variations on Voice*. "What every woman knows but rarely discusses. I don't mind erasure if it is done by my own hand."

She looks at its shades of meaning—to rub out, to eliminate completely, to obliterate, to murder. The word comes from the Latin; it shares a root with *raze*.

Williams writes in pencil and uses an eraser. But even then, doesn't a trace remain?

The Moving Finger writes; and, having writ,
Moves on: nor all thy Piety nor Wit
Shall lure it back to cancel half a Line,
Nor all thy Tears wash out a Word of it.

~~You cannot erase a growth. You can excise it, but it is cut—not rubbed—away.~~ Something is missing. An absence is left. What will you fill it with? What substance? What story?

When the Great Salt Lake rose to a record high of nearly 4,212 feet and spread to cover almost 2,400 square miles, it didn't think, What about the birds in the Bear River Refuge? The tracks of the Southern Pacific Railroad? The needs of a daughter losing her mother too soon, too soon?

When a development takes over a hillside, it doesn't think, What about the land beneath us? The trees we have felled? The animals we have displaced? The water we have diverted?

~~When a nodule grows on a thyroid it doesn't think, What about the airway I might threaten? The pressure I might cause? The possibility of cancer I inject?~~

As almost a joke I unfolded a bird guide—a laminated sheet of maybe fifty one-inch birds—and asked, "Where's the robin?" My daughter, two years and two months old, looked and looked and looked and pointed. Robin. She was right.

"A mother and a daughter are an edge," Williams writes.

A sharp edge can cut: the edge of a knife, the edge of a sheet of paper. A round edge smooths the transition from one plane to another: the curve of a torso from ventral to dorsal, the lip of a bowl from inside to out. Regardless of its shape, an edge divides and defines: mother/daughter, healthy/stricken, grafting/pruning, living/dying.

The twins—my daughters—will live beyond me. Their lives are wide open, and they don't know agoraphobia. My life is not claustrophobic, but it has narrowed narrowed narrowed with each choice.

There's a danger in living vicariously through your children, but— when they are small—it is impossible to live separate, parallel. We are in this—this life, this dyad, this ecotone—together. I cannot live for them or through them, but I can witness and fuel and follow and lead.

Today I spent an hour listening to recordings of birdsongs. I want to tell them black-capped chickadee and white-throated sparrow and Carolina wren when they ask.

Once you open your ears to birdsong, it is everywhere.

The return of robins forecasts spring. A robin in a bird guide invites identification, learning, a choice made, a path taken, pride.

Birds are sent from ships to shore; canaries are lowered into mines; falcons are loosed to find prey; needles pierce the body to extract an answer.

~~Four needles, thirty seconds each, in a deep node more than half an inch in. One can think of this with wonder—that so much knowledge can be drawn from such a simple procedure. One can think of this with fear—that four needles will strike, twitch, jerk, push, and draw both blood and bruise. One can try not to think of it at all, to forget once it's happened, to refuse to count the days as 48 hours stretches into a week.~~

The raven was sent away and never came back. Did it drown? Did it find land and stay there? What of its mate back in the ark?

The dove returned with an olive branch and, presumably, reunited with its mate. But what of the raven?

The dove came back with a story in its beak. The raven disappeared into silence. When we have flown alone over deep waters, what story do we tell when we return? What stories do those left behind tell if we do not?

~~It will take a weekend to absorb the knowledge that my story, for now, stops here.~~

~~It will take two weeks for the coin-sized bruise in the hollow of my throat to fade from plum to glaucous to yellow to white.~~

~~It will take longer than that to believe that my body has finally absorbed the blood and the bruise is gone.~~

~~It will take longer still for me to conclude with "The End."~~

Are those wings on the horizon? A branch in the beak? Doubt grows in silence and in stealth, while hope circles for a perch.

Assemblage

Raw Materials

To make history, gather together a poet, his lover, another poet, and his doctor. Send them on a summer vacation but have the weather betray them, turn cold and wet, keep them inside near a roaring fire. Provide a book of ghost stories and a spirit of competition. One of them, the lover, Mary Shelley, will write *Frankenstein*.

history: ORIGIN Late Middle English,
via Latin from Greek *historia*, "finding out"

To make a creature, start by stalking the dead. Dig them up and take what you need. Assemble the parts according to your ideals: strength, symmetry, beauty. Apply what science you have learned over sleepless nights and fevered days. Behold your creation—and be dismayed.

dismay: ORIGIN Middle English, based on Latin *dis-*,
"expressing negation" + the Germanic base of *may*,
from a base meaning "have power"

To make meat, kill the animal. If it is a lamb, one shot between the eyes will do. When you strip the skin, the room will smell like sex, your hands burnished by fat. When you cut through the abdomen, the organs will spill out onto the floor, the stomach bloating as you watch. When you saw through the spine, you will think of Frankenstein and his nighttime labors.

labor: ORIGIN Middle English *labo(u)r*,
from Latin *labor*, "toil, trouble"

To make a child, you need an egg and a sperm. But there is more violence to it. The follicle ruptures when the egg is released, leaving remnants called a corpus luteum. If the egg remains unfertilized, the corpus luteum degenerates into scar tissue. If fertilized, the division and then multiplication of cells begins. This continues through labor and birth until the fetus is incarnate.

incarnate: ORIGIN Late Middle English, from Ecclesiastical
Latin *incarnat-*, "made flesh," from the verb *incarnare*,
from *in-*, "into" + *caro, carn-*, "flesh"

There's always a little carnage in creation.

Head

Letters

To the Sister I Never Had (Never Knew I Had):

How difficult it has been to find a balance between caring for the creations of my body and the creations of my mind.

Frankenstein starts with a letter from the explorer Walton to his sister back in England. Walton writes of his ambitions, his desire to discover hospitable land beyond the North Pole. Instead, he finds Victor Frankenstein.

But, of course, I do not have a sister. If you were my secret twin, you were absorbed back into wherever we came from before I was born alone.

And now I have twins.

I am ambitious—like Walton, like Frankenstein—to explore, to discover, to create.

Frankenstein chose the creation of his mind. It was his research, his scientific experiments, his defiant intellect, and his brutal determination that led him to create life not from his body but from his laboratory. He kept a journal of his accomplishments, but the reader of Frankenstein does not get to read it. Only his creature does.

I keep a journal too:

> Washington DC, July 5, 20—.
> I'm pregnant.
> That looks so stark. I'm pregnant! That's better—and closer to how I feel.

(Even then, barely pregnant enough to show the second line on the stick, I was struggling to fit the expectations of what we require a mother to be.)

> Washington DC, July 28, 20—.
> Twins.

(That's all I wrote in my journal that day and for many days thereafter—aside from a quote from No Country for Old Men: "All the time you spend trying to get back what's been took from you, more is going out the door."

I couldn't manage the door. I could not fathom a life—as a writer, as a person—as a mother of twins. I was convinced they—two against one—would be my undoing. I was completely dismayed.)

Will my twins ever read these words, as Frankenstein's creature did? Will they understand the powers and responsibilities of creation? Or will they unravel my life, as the creature does Frankenstein's?

Myths

Once upon a time in Geneva, in the eighteenth century, there was a little boy named Victor Frankenstein who grew up being told he could do anything. He created a life that killed everyone he loved.

Once upon a time in America, in the middle of the twentieth century, there was a generation of girls who were told they could have it all. They killed themselves trying to acquire it.

Once upon a time, a very long time ago, there was a rebellious angel who was cast out of heaven. How many died from his downfall?

Once upon a time, not all that long ago, there was a different kind of angel—what Virginia Woolf called the "Angel in the House," the ideal image of a Victorian wife and mother. Woolf wrote, "Killing the Angel in the House was part of the occupation of a woman writer."

Frames

Who tells your story?

Frankenstein is told through a set of nesting narratives, each a matryoshka doll within the next. First Walton's, then Frankenstein's, and then—at the very center—the creature's, told with an eloquence that will surprise a first-time reader expecting the movie monster's grunts and groans. This creature has read Milton, Plutarch, and Goethe, and these stories help shape the way he sees the world. They teach him about responsibility and betrayal, ego and exile, love and loss.

What stories shape a creator's world? For Victor Frankenstein it was alchemy and science, but nothing prepared him for the creature's need.

What stories shape a mother's world? What stories can teach her about desire and duty, self and other, person and parent? *The Scarlet Letter*? *Anna Karenina*? *Sophie's Choice*? *Medea*? None of these stories show me a version of motherhood I want to live. Neither does *Frankenstein*. But this story alone shows me the agony of creation—of creations. The struggle of how to care for the creations of your body without neglecting the creations of your mind.

Heart

The human heart has four chambers. Half of them need oxygen; the other half are full of it.

Victor. His need, his oxygen, is the creation of beauty.	Victor's friend Clerval. His heart beats poetry.
The creature. His need is love.	Elizabeth, Victor's adopted sister and later his bride. Her heart beats love— for everyone.

Guts

To have guts is to be brave. To spill your guts is to tell your innermost secrets. To have a gut feeling is to know beyond knowledge.

There's a newfound connection between your guts and your mind, what you eat and how you think, the bacteria you harbor and the mood that harbors you.

A pregnancy happens not in your gut but in a place no less visceral. It doesn't care what you think or how you feel, what you eat—only that you do. Those cells keep dividing, multiplying, with no interference from your mind or will. All that growth happens in the dark.

Hands

Hands create in the light. They are of the body, but they can do the mind's work.

These hands held *Frankenstein* in a hotel room far from home while these eyes read, jealously, about Walton's voyage and Frankenstein's research, their freedom to pursue, single-mindedly, one committed passion.

These hands held *Frankenstein* on a sick child's bed while these eyes read—heartbroken—about the creature confronting the creator who had abandoned him: "I am thy creature; I ought to be thy Adam; but I am rather the fallen angel, whom thou drivest from joy for no misdeed." And then these hands put the book down, cared for the sick child who had been sleeping in that bed, and didn't pick up the book again for days.

How to weigh the work of the hands against the work of the gut, the work of the head against the work of the heart? Victor Frankenstein fled his creation as soon as it began to need, but I cannot flee mine.

I can cast out the Angel in my House again and again—but I cannot cast out my Adams. Nor can I cast out my writing. In choosing one, I am inherently neglecting the other. There are days when this feels like a butchering—half myself cut away or something unwanted stitched to me. A cleaving either way.

But I do not abandon my creations. I will live my story and tell it too. I will keep faith with my work, trust that the spark will come, the words stir. I will remind myself that I am the assembler—and raw materials are everywhere.

Vertebrae

From one angle it looks like
an iris. From another
a rocket ship.

Or a dinosaur, with a crest
rising from the center plane
of its face.

Or a snapdragon. Or a heart.

Not an anatomical heart but
a stylized one, two curved
lobes meeting at a point
at the bottom.

It is easy, at first, to see only
the abstract, to forget that
this was once part of a living
animal.

But there is the tunnel where
its spinal cord once was,
a cord that bound it
to movement, to life.

There are the fledgling
beginnings of ribs.

There are other hooks
and flares that kept this bone
attached
to muscles, tendons, other
bones.

What happens when all
attachments fall away
and you are left only
with this?

When the twins were born
a doctor shot an anesthetic
in the space between two
vertebrae.

I tried not to think too hard
about this. It's a common
thing. But still, but still.

It was a sliver of metal,
a push of opiates. And then
the twins were cut free.

Having a spine makes me
a particular animal—not an
insect, not an octopus.

Having a backbone makes me
a particular person—not
a pushover, not
a milquetoast. But. But.

I recently said to my husband,
No. My camel's back is
already broken.

That last straw is just a bier
along with all those that came
before it.

I gnaw at the meat
of my circumstance until there
is only this, clean picked,
guarded,
worried over.

I could say I have a bone
to pick with the turn my life
has taken.

I could say
I am bone-tired.

That I have worked myself to
the bone.

This vertebra is bone-dry, but
once it and its others were full
of fluid.

The deer around it stood
and walked and leaped
and drank and curled to sleep
in a nest of tall grasses.

What drew me to this thing,
this internal private thing
I should not be allowed
to tumble in my hands?

What draws me to strip away
what's tender, to get
to the bone?

I wonder what a living spine
feels like.

Wet, flexible, hard, tensile,
able.

An iris. A snapdragon.
An abstract heart.
Mine.

IV

The Voice at the Window

Yet Another Day at the Jersey Shore

After the mourning doves cooed, my grandmother got up and started breakfast. I woke to the click of plates, the metallic scrape of a frying pan on a gas burner. Under my bed was a vent with an ornate cast-iron grate that looked down into the dining room. Sometimes I would slide under the bed so I could look down at the toaster and a corner of the dining room table. No one ever had any interesting conversations in the dining room after my bedtime or just before breakfast, but I liked the idea of spying through the grate so much that I would sometimes slide under the bed just to watch the toast pop up.

My grandmother was a believer in full breakfasts. She made fried or scrambled eggs, sometimes pancakes or French toast. There was always sausage or bacon and toast or English muffins with butter, jam, and marmalade. I learned to like marmalade because it was always on the breakfast table. There was always a small glass of milk and a small glass of orange juice by each plate. And coffee or tea. Napkins and all the appropriate silverware. I loved these breakfasts. At home it was usually cold cereal with milk. Unsweetened too.

After breakfast I walked down to the Little Kids' Beach. Our family called it that because it was a small bay beach, tame compared to the ocean. Little kids could swim there without getting crushed by the waves at high tide. There was a playground at this beach, which I liked more than the bay itself, even though the slide turned deadly in the noontime sun and the high dark monkey bars burned your hands on the long way across. There were also swings with long chains that swung you really, really high, and if you threw yourself out at the highest point, the sand would cushion your fall.

There was a dock at the Little Kids' Beach that I liked to sit on but could not make myself jump off. A slick green rope studded with Styrofoam buoys marked the boundary of the swimming area. Beyond this rope was a finger of Barnegat Bay and the coastline of Lavallette. Boats idled wakeless in the water, slowly chugging or drifting to their moorings. We weren't allowed to swim out there.

I didn't want to swim much of anywhere. The bay was cloudy and salty, and when you were only a foot deep, your feet started to look lifeless and strange. After a yard you couldn't see the bottom at all. And there were crabs. Once I saw one swimming awkwardly beside me, and its lurching claws were enough to panic me back to shore. Sometimes I swam out to the buoy line and held onto one of the Styrofoam balls, but I was always uneasy, looking out for flailing crabs, ghostly fish, or whatever other dark things might lurk in the bay.

Going to the ocean beach was a production. Grandpa packed our gear in the enormous trunk of his pale yellow Cadillac: always a big beach umbrella, always beach chairs for him and Grandma, always towels, and, for them, always hats. My grandfather wore the same hat whenever he went to the ocean beach. It was made of woven palm fronds, and to cool himself off, he would dip it in the ocean, wait for the water to run out in streams, and put it back on his head. My grandfather was quite bald by then and usually wore a golf cap. But at the beach he wore his hat of fronds. My grandmother had a thick head of salt-and-pepper hair. She wore a white bubble hat with multicolor bows sewn to it. Sometimes she wore a white bathing cap studded with white rubber flowers. I was fascinated by this cap, but I never could decide if I actually liked it or not.

Once the car was packed, we would drive up to President Avenue. This was considered the best beach, but it was really the same beach as all the others, just a block or so up the coast. But my grandparents thought it was the best, so that's where we went. All the avenues—Ortley, New Brunswick, Reese, Vance—dead-ended into the boardwalk, and the beach was just beyond that. Each avenue had a weathered wooden shelter with benches all along its frame and a pay phone to call for your ride if you needed one. I didn't need a ride, though, because I was with my grandparents.

Grandpa let me pick our spot, which wasn't too close to the water, where the tide might come in, but it wasn't too close to the boardwalk either, where the sand was so hot I understood how it could be used to make glass. Grandpa set up the umbrella with an *oomp* sound, put a chair under it for Grandma and one beside it for himself. He kicked off his slides and skinned off his shirt and went straight "for a dip." I was always impressed to see him bobbing out past the wave line, something I thought took great bravery.

Grandma settled into her chair with a book or maybe the paper. She liked to do the crossword puzzle and other word games—the scrambled words in Jumble, the hidden words in a grid of letters. There was always a *Family Circus* cartoon on the same page. I often puzzled over these cartoons, not knowing how they were supposed to be funny. Grandma never really swam. Sometimes she walked into the ocean up to her thighs and then splashed herself with water, but that was it.

The ocean felt both safe and scary to me. It felt safer then the Little Kids' Beach because everything was so churned up by the waves that you rarely saw crabs in the water. But all this churning was scary too. It took me a while to navigate the waves, to know when to jump over them and when it was better to hold my nose and duck under, trusting that there wouldn't be another wave right behind it to crush me when I emerged.

Once after an ordeal with the waves, I wrapped myself completely in one of the big red-and-blue spiral print towels, lay down, pulled a corner over my face, and closed my eyes. I pretended to be a mummy in the desert sands, slowly letting the heat of the sun warm me back to life. After a little while I opened my eyes. I could see the sun in little squares through the weave of the towel, slanting through the terrycloth in tiny shafts of light. But then I saw a squiggly shape float by—and then another. Atoms, I thought. I'm seeing atoms. Finally, my secret superhero talent was revealed! I watched the atoms float by all afternoon. That evening I told my dad because he could be trusted with such weighty revelations. "They're not atoms," he told me. "They're cells." At first I was disappointed, but then I thought that cells were really small too. Not as small as atoms but still really, really small. But then he said that everyone could see them if the conditions were right—if you could trick your eye into focusing on its own surface instead of what lay beyond it. It took me awhile to let go of the fantasy that I was unique in my ability to see cells, if not atoms, and even now, when the conditions are right and I see the same squiggly shapes float across my line of vision, I wonder what superhero lives just below my mortal skin.

At the beach I found myself able to watch the pattern of waves for longer than I ever could have sat still at home. I dug holes and collected shells and watched the sandpipers furiously trotting back and forth along the foam the waves left behind or watched the tiny air bubbles pop up from the sleeping clams farther below the surface than I had ever cared to dig. Or I would walk over to the lifeguard stand and check the temperature of the air and water or the times for high and low tide. Once I cut my foot on a piece of broken glass, and I limped over to the lifeguard's chair to get a Band-Aid. The lifeguard was extra nice, and somehow I knew he was flirting with me, even though I was just a kid and didn't care one way or the other if he was. Another time, after applying some ancient tanning accelerator I had found in a closet, I waited anxiously for my skin to turn black and peel off. Disappointingly, nothing happened.

Sometime during the afternoon I would hear the bell of the ice cream truck and pick my way across the hot sand, the perilous boardwalk, where one misplaced scuff of the foot could bring slivers the size of sewing needles, and finally the searing asphalt. Even at the end of the summer I was still a tenderfoot; there was no way to pass as a townie with my wincing steps and pale skin, no matter how salty and faded my Lavallette sweatshirts were. But the call of the truck was strong, and I rarely failed to answer. I'd have a dollar in change clutched in my fist as I stood on first one foot and then the other. If I was lucky, I could walk along one of the cooler yellow lines painted at the end of the street, but the truck always seemed to park just beyond their reach. I thought that there was only one ice cream truck that drove up and down the whole coastline of New Jersey selling the traditional red-white-and-blue rocket pops; and the candy version, Astro Pops; and the ice cream bars with crunchy bits sprinkled all over them—strawberry shortcake and toasted almond bars, which I only grew to like when I got older.

I was always tired after a day at the ocean. There was something about the sun and the waves that dried and drained me, even if I had barely moved from my towel. In the late afternoon Grandpa disassembled our camp, and we trudged back toward the car. First there was the hot sand studded with cigarette butts and splintery popsicle sticks and twists of straw wrappers. Then there was the transfer from sand to boardwalk when the flip-flops or sandals would go on and trap the gritty sand against my skin.

The dark interior of the car let loose shimmering waves when Grandpa opened the door. But there was something infinitely comforting about those dark-blue velvet seats; it seemed the exact opposite of the bright sandy beach, and as I sank into them, the soft warmth heated my legs and back like a bath. The sand seemed to seep through this velvet membrane and disappear, and as the automatic air conditioner clicked on and blew still-warm air through the car, I grew sleepy, even though it was only a five-minute drive home. It was so dark in the back seat that I now wonder if the windows were tinted, but I think it was just the contrast of the white sun, the pale pebbled yards, and the heat rising from the asphalt that made that warm blue velvet nest a safer, darker haven.

When we got home, we took showers. Often I would have to wait until last, and I sat, gritty, on the couch downstairs. I held the brown-and-yellow-and-white turtle pillow in my lap and felt the sand in my waistband, between my toes, behind my knees—anywhere one part of my body touched another. My hair was sticky with salt and, at that age, usually hung in a ratty ponytail or fraying braid.

Grandpa's big brown La-Z-Boy faced the door, and Grandma's red wool recliner sat next to it. In front of them was the TV and a fireplace I never saw used. On the mantle were wooden duck decoys and a statue of a crusty old sea captain in a yellow coat, blue pants, and white hat. He had a pipe molded onto the side of his face, and a red coal glowed in the end of it. He looked sly. Years later, when my grandfather died and we had to go through the house, this sly captain was the one thing I asked for. At the foot of the stairs was a woodpecker door knocker screwed into the wall. I would always flip it, ticktock, when I went upstairs. Against the wall where the stairs disappeared was the couch I sat on, holding the turtle pillow. On top of the coffee table was a milk glass bowl with a lid. Inside that bowl were hard butterscotch candies or Werther's caramels.

Eventually it was my turn to climb the stairs—ticktock went the woodpecker—leaving grains of sand that would accumulate in the corners like white dust.

The bathroom was tiny; only one person could use it at a time. I took great pleasure in peeling off my damp and sticky suit, revealing faint tan lines and often the harsh imprint of the elastic straps and leg holes. At eight I was wearing a bright-orange tank with a nubbly butt from sitting on curbs, sidewalks, docks, pool edges, and the sandy bottom of the ocean. I balled the suit up in a sink full of cool water, and my skin sang in the warm air.

Over the sink was a smallish round mirror, and directly opposite it, over the toilet, was a medicine cabinet with a mirrored door. These two mirrors reflected endless images of yourself as you stood between them. I thought you could see into infinity with these mirrors, but it was always too blurry to be satisfying.

There was strange stuff in the medicine cabinet above the toilet. Bright blue bottles of aftershave, a tired toothbrush with a white opaque handle, chalky tablets of antacid, and long tubes of denture glue— nothing I ever used but all things I would look through on a regular basis, just to see if anything was used up or added. Nothing ever was.

My grandmother had a cake of Ivory soap in the shower, another by the sink. Once I filled the sink with water to see if Ivory soap really floated. It did. At home we used Dove, also white but an oval, not a rectangle. There was something solid in that square bar that I turned over and over in my hands, trying to whittle it down to that familiar oval, but always it balked me. I liked that it did. I used hot water in the shower even when it was hot outside. I felt cleaner.

When I was done, I put on fresh clothes and padded downstairs for cocktails—not for me, for my grandparents.

My grandfather sat in his chair with a drink sweating into the coaster on the table beside him. He had a scotch with ice and maybe water, or maybe the ice made the water. My grandmother drank scotch, too, but I had iced tea that my grandmother made from a mix, dusty scoopfuls she pulled from a big yellow canister and then dumped into the teal pitcher she always used for iced tea. Tea dust would rise from the pitcher, and if I leaned in too close, I would cough.

Then there was the snack dish of Planters peanuts or cheese curls. My grandfather always had peanuts, but sometimes he would pinch a curl from my dish. He would watch golf in the afternoons—how did there always seem to be golf on in the afternoons?—and I would be bored. If Grandma was making dinner, I would sit in her chair. If she was in her chair, then I would relegate myself to the couch and the flowered turtle pillow. Maybe I read while my grandfather watched golf—or maybe he watched the local news. Maybe I just watched him watch. The cheese curls were enough.

The dining room had busy wallpaper—medallions of eagles in red, white, and a weirdly turquoise blue. There was always a tablecloth on the table, a plastic one that you could sweep clean with a scrubby-backed sponge. There was the toaster on its small table in the corner and on the wall above it a painting by my aunt Linda of a sailboat in a bay. There was a seagull flying across the sky in this painting that I always thought was a fish jumping high out of the water. But my dad said, no, it was a seagull. I never was fully convinced.

The kitchen had turquoise painted cabinets and odd melamine dishes—castoffs from other houses, other times. Teacups hung from hooks in the pantry, and a cake plate with a metal cover sat on top of the refrigerator. To turn the overhead light on, you pulled a cord that had a red plastic apple on the end of it. For a long time I couldn't reach it.

Dinner was always substantial. There was always a meat, always a vegetable, always a dessert. The dessert was usually a thick slice of yellow cake from the covered plate on top of the fridge. My grandfather had coffee or tea afterward and then watched more TV or read one of his thick crime novels while lying in his easy chair in a circle of yellow lamplight. My grandmother liked to watch game shows like *Jeopardy* and *Wheel of Fortune*. She had a thing for Vanna White. "Va-va-va-Vanna," my grandmother would say, when Vanna appeared in yet another evening gown. It was the kind of thing said just to take up space, just to put sound in the air. It was the kind of thing my grandparents often said.

Maybe I read or watched TV. I don't remember doing much of anything—just being—in the warm yellow light of the living room, the ducks on the mantle, the few inescapable grains of sand under my elbows as I lay on the couch. The smell of dinner served and lemon dish soap lingered in the air along with the occasional clink of a cup in a saucer, the soft turn of a page. I often tried to sneak candies from their milk glass dish, but the crackly wrappers made it hard.

After my grandmother washed the dishes and set them to dry in the rack, after she toweled them off and placed them back on the pantry shelves, after she sponged off the dining room tablecloth with the yellow scrubby-backed sponge, then and only then would I take down a box from the shelf in the closet and we would play a game.

Sometimes it was Scrabble. My grandmother was great at Scrabble. She almost always won, but she was always nice about it. She even turned a blind eye to my cheating. I would take out the dictionary, claiming that I needed to double-check the spelling of a word, and then feverishly look for words that started with Q and didn't need a U or words that began with X or Z. "No," I would say casually while my eyes still worked the page. "No," I would stall as I tried to eke out one more word. "No," I would say, slowly closing the cover. "I guess it wasn't spelled that way after all." This strategy rarely resulted in a word I could play, and my grandmother surely knew this. Or maybe she saw this as a fair way to even the field between an eight-year-old and a sixty-three-year-old. I remember her pointed pearly fingernails against the square tiles, the wood darkened through time and the touch of many fingertips. I remember her round glasses and how she looked both through them and above them. I remember the first time I played, when I laid down my first word diagonally—I was no fool; look at all the points I could pick up!—until she told me, gently, that they had to be vertical or horizontal. I'm sure there are still score sheets in that old box—where is it now?—with an R for *Randon* versus a G for *Grandma*.

Sometimes we played Yahtzee. This I liked better—because there was more chance to it. Grandma would blow on the dice and chant, "I need a Yahtzee!" as she swirled the dice in the cup. Whenever either of us would get a great roll, we would cry out, "Oh! There's that full house," "There's four of a kind," "There's—I can't believe it—Yahtzee!" We were both generous in our wins, although I don't think I was as graceful in defeat. The inside of that Yahtzee cup had such a distinctive smell. Once a Band-Aid straight from the wrapper smelled just like that Yahtzee cup. Once—disturbingly—my armpit. Once, years later, the back of a taxicab.

Outside the circle of light the dining room lamp cast over the table, the kitchen was dark. In the back of the kitchen was the back door, the washing machine, a closet for storage, and an even smaller closet that hid a toilet. This toilet could save you a trip upstairs, but it was very cramped. At night it was also very dark, especially when you weren't tall enough to reach the apple cord that hung from the kitchen light. The window above the washing machine was black and shiny; you couldn't tell if someone was right outside looking in or if what you saw was your own reflection. You could leave the door open and block the window, which also gave you more room for your knees, but then you risked discovery by someone coming into the kitchen for a snack.

After games and maybe a last slice of cake with milk, I would go to bed. Once again I would climb the stairs—ticktock, woodpecker—and brush my teeth in the little bathroom, skip washing my face because I could get away with it, and head to bed.

The sign over my grandparent's bedroom door said CAPTAIN'S QUARTERS. The sign over the other bedroom said CREW'S QUARTERS. My grandparents' bedroom was green but not a pleasant one. It was a green with a lot of yellow in it. I didn't spend a lot of time in this room, but I remember two twin beds, which I thought was strange and kind of sad, although I didn't know exactly why.

The other bedroom—my bedroom when I visited alone—was the Crew's Quarters. The wallpaper in this room had pen-and-ink drawings of ships and eagles. It was so old that you could draw on it with your fingernail and the lines you carved into its ivory surface would show up the color of cardboard. I tried to limit my fingernail's patterns because I didn't want to get caught. Often I would stop at just one dent, almost hidden on the border of an eagle's wing or a ship's hull. It was a compulsion.

The sheets on the two twin beds were red-white-and-blue striped. There was a wooden dresser with flowers painted on the knobs—a castoff from Aunt Linda's girlhood bedroom—and a closet with the same shuttered doors as the downstairs porch. There was a dormer window in the center of the room, and each bed lay under the steep slant of the roof on either side. There was another window near the foot of the bed that had a little half-circle of metal that you could twist and then open the screen into the room like a door.

I liked to sleep with the windows open. I could hear the breeze in the sills and the rope of the flagpole dinging like sail ropes against a mast. The dull silvery light from the streetlamp outside cast flat gray shadows and made the room look like an old-fashioned movie. Later, when I read James Joyce's short story "The Dead," I recognized the same quality of light on Gretta's skirt as she stood in the hall listening to "The Lass of Aughrim." But now the wind whistled like a ghost, and the closet doors almost started to open as a car's headlights swept the room. But then the light would become a warmer gray, so warm it was almost a pale yellow, and the flag's rope would swing against the pole in the day's early breeze, and the doves would coo in another morning.

Down in the kitchen, as Grandma started another pot of coffee, the calendar that hung behind the pantry door never seemed to change. Even as Grandpa flipped the page at the end of each month, the pictures always seemed the same—seagulls, sailboats, sunsets. Every month the tides were advertised, high and low, and the same ads offered seafood dinners and beachwear, and each square held the same blank possibility of yet another day at the Jersey Shore.

The Sparkling Future

B and I had been together for a little over a year, balanced on that fine point where the slightest inclination—a breath of feeling—would push us into forever or nothing. We were standing on a bridge over the Kennebec River in Maine when I realized this. The phrase entered my head whole but uninvited, as if someone had swooped down to whisper it in my ear, and I played with it, turning it over and over in my mind until, like an engine, it caught life. That fine point. Forever. Nothing. Now that this thought had come to me, what would I do about it?

It was summertime. Beneath our feet the river swelled and raged, swallowed itself and spat back up. Tree branches and chunks of Styrofoam and other trash thrashed through the water, curling around the rocks before being swept away to the unknown, to the sea.

I leaned into B, my back against his chest; breathed into him as his arms, as if by habit, encircled my waist. There was comfort there. He was always warm, even when it was coldest, and I steeped myself in his warmth as if in a hot bath. But there was something wrong, some tinge, some tint of distance even as I laced my fingers through his, my palms over the backs of his hands. How could this turn into nothing? But forever . . . ?

We had fought the night before in our hotel room, each sitting on one queen bed, the headboards facing each other like mirrored images. I had laughed when we first saw the beds. A bed a night, I joked. But we only slept in the first, uneasily, after I squirmed away from his touch, after I apologized and cried, apologized again, not sure what for but it seemed the thing to do, his voice frustrated, mine turning from regret to anger, until I suddenly sat up and wrenched the covers from the end of our bed, wrapped up, and faced him, left naked, startled, dark, and alone against the smooth white sheet.

"What," I demanded, "do you want from me?" He couldn't answer, of course, but he didn't have to. His answer was mine. Everything and nothing. The next day, on the bridge, I remembered and weighed.

We had met in New York, in graduate school, in the English department. It was early fall, and he was tan from the summer sun. His teeth were perfect—white and square—and his easy smile lit up his hazel eyes. His head was round, and his high forehead seemed to showcase the brain behind it. I was immediately glamoured.

During that first meeting we talked while draped over the couches and stuffed chairs in the department lounge. Then we had lunch in the East Village at the Rose of India underneath Christmas tree lights and tinsel, even though it was September. Occasionally we met for coffee, sometimes dinner. We prowled used bookstores and watched three-card monte games on street corners and looked at antique fountain pens at the Chelsea Flea Market. At night we called each other, talking for hours without realizing hours had passed; once one of us saw that it was already five thirty in the morning, so he rollerbladed up Broadway to meet me for breakfast. We talked about the books we read. We compared notes about our professors and gossiped about our fellow students. We talked about our future plans to get doctorate degrees, postdoc fellowships, travel grants, Fulbrights, and then perfect teaching jobs at small liberal arts colleges where we could live in white colonials with gardens out back. Or maybe we would stay in New York and have river-view apartments with balconies full of potted herbs and a membership at the Met. Or maybe we'd move to Paris—or Prague. Anything was possible.

Then, as fall edged toward winter, I went over to his apartment for dinner. After the spaghetti and candlelight, after we had talked ourselves out, it was too late for me to go home. He said he'd sleep on the floor and hugged me good night. But this was not a street-corner hug, a just-outside-the-apartment-door hug, a see-you-later hug. We were inside, alone in his bedroom. Suddenly it was very hot, and the wool of his sweater stuck to my cheek, and my body prickled with sweat, and even though I didn't want to, I had to let go; I was dizzy, reeling. This was not the moment I was hoping for. As I drew back, he kissed me on the cheek, a kiss that was meant to be the beginning of so much more, but my vision was tunneling, and I knew I was about to faint. I was wrecking our moment. I remember meaning to say, "I'm sorry, but I'm going to pass out now," but only getting as far as "I'm sorry, but—" before my vision grayed over and my knees buckled. I wasn't sick, it wasn't food poisoning, and I wasn't the fainting type. But the next thing I knew I was lying on the floor, half-supported by his arm, his warm hazel eyes looking down at me with fascination and something else. What man could resist the power of making a woman swoon with a kiss? And what woman could fail to succumb to that power? Not him, not me.

Our first summer together was full of small adventures—wandering through obscure museum exhibits, hiking in Upstate New York, kayaking in New Jersey, riding the Wonder Wheel and the Scrambler at Coney Island. But summer also brought our first fights—about a cache of *Playboys* I discovered in his bedroom, about his flirtations and my jealousies, about the way we treated each other's families, about ex-girlfriends and ex-boyfriends who wrote or called or showed up unexpectedly and what we did or didn't do about them. In the fall he worked on his dissertation on childlessness in early American literature while I wrote papers for Elizabethan Drama and Introduction to Middle English. Winter brought head colds and a letter from his most significant ex, the one he had thought he might marry, the one, it turned out, he had broken up with only days before we met. This led to a rash of new arguments and reconciliations between cafés and classes and movies and walks around the city. But still, in those cold winter months, our reconciliations were as heated as our fights. By spring, though, we were in limbo—he hadn't gotten a teaching job, and I hadn't gotten into a PhD program. All our talk about fellowships and grants and our bright, sparkling future evaporated. We didn't know where we'd be in the fall or if we'd be together. Summertime would bring the answer.

Back on the bridge I said, "Let's go," and we clung to the rails to try to get back to where we were before, back to the bank and the car and the road. Stepping off the bridge, we felt the ground pitch beneath us but couldn't laugh at our staggering—not yet. It wasn't until we were back on the highway that the talk spilled from us: *Wow*, it began. *Can you imagine? Swimming in that? Or trying to?* We were still charged by what we had seen and felt on the bridge.

The next morning was humid, rainy, and the glass of the car fogged up as we sat in the parking lot behind our hotel. My coffee sat in the cup holder, steam curling between us, ready for the long drive home.

"It's not for that long," he said.

"Just the summer," I said.

"And then we'll both be back in New York."

He kissed me goodbye and left. I drove home, back down Route 95, through New Hampshire, around Boston, and down again through Upstate New York, trying to frame what had happened, trying to find words and phrases that fit, and realized that I would have to wait. Wait and see if he would end it when I couldn't, or if, after all, I could.

He was the one, two months later, who made the call.

I had been in London for three weeks. I was a teaching assistant for a Shakespeare class in a study abroad program for American students. I lived in a single room in John Dodgson House with a balcony overlooking Bidborough Street. I spent my mornings in the classroom, with its oak desks and creaky chairs, and my afternoons under the bright lights of the reading room of the British Library and, throughout the day, drank far too much tea—out of china, out of porcelain, and out of Styrofoam cups. I was in love with the city, the country and its history.

I had gone to graduate school to study Renaissance drama and fed myself not only with plays by Shakespeare, Marlowe, Kyd, and Webster but also with stories about Lady Jane Grey, queen for only nine days before being executed for treason; Mary Tudor, nicknamed "Bloody Mary" for the many Protestant heretics she executed; Elizabeth I and her own precarious rise to power, the fatal rivalry between her and Mary, Queen of Scots, and her own Parliament's numerous attempts to see her safely married to produce an heir for England. But I was especially fascinated by the history that preceded and informed all of this: the story of Henry VIII and his many wives.

"Divorced, beheaded, died; divorced, beheaded, survived." This is the rhyme I learned to keep them straight. Catherine of Aragon, Anne Boleyn, Jane Seymour, Anne of Cleves, Katherine Howard, and Catherine Parr. But the wife who fascinated me the most was the second one, Anne Boleyn, the one who caused such a burning fascination in the king that he divorced his first wife, Catherine of Aragon, to marry her.

This is the wife I would have wanted to be. "Anne of a thousand days," she was called. But what days! She captivated the king through her dark good looks—her brown hair, her black eyes, her slim neck and slight build. Thomas Wyatt called her "Brunet" in his poetry, describing her as "wild for to hold," though she seemed tame. This wildness intrigued the king—she had a keen mind and a sharp tongue and a quick temper—and she kept him in pursuit by constantly twisting away from his sexual advances; she refused to be his mistress. Within a year of their meeting, the king decided that it was his destiny to have a second chance in life: he would put away his first wife, marry Anne Boleyn, and start a new family.

This is the power that I admired—the power to captivate a man, to enchant him, to posses him so fully that he thought of little else. Henry had been married to Catherine for eighteen years. They had a daughter, Mary, and had mourned the deaths of their other five children; Catherine had been seriously ill, and Henry had been badly shaken by a jousting accident; together they had faced war with France and attacks from Scotland and intrigues and rebellions within their own court. But now Catherine was in her forties, five years older than Henry, and her plump blonde prettiness had faded into something broad and bland. She was wise, loyal, and still very much in love with Henry, but she was a given—not a challenge to be met or a game to be won. Anne Boleyn was just that—a challenge, a game—and because the outcome was far from certain, Henry played all the harder. To cast this kind of capricious power over the most powerful man in England—the king—must have been for Anne another kind of seduction, where you seduce yourself into believing that, with your charm and skill and ability, anything is possible.

This is the power I had wanted to wield over B—and had, briefly, in the first few months of our relationship. Just before we met, he had broken up with the woman he had thought he would marry; she was blonde, loving, and solid, as I imagined Catherine must have been. In her youth Catherine was described as plump and pretty, with red-gold hair and a bright complexion. Her chosen motto was "Humble and Loyal," her badge a pomegranate. (In contrast, Anne Boleyn's badge was a falcon, her daring motto "The Most Happy.") An early portrait shows Catherine's eyes demurely downcast despite her elaborate headdress; in a later one her mouth is set—as if to confirm her stubborn loyalty to the king. All her life she was praised for her coloring—her creamy complexion and honey-colored hair—but a poet could have called me "Brunet." I was slim and sharp, fair-skinned and dark-eyed, with long dark hair I could toss over my shoulder after a fight. I fancied myself a passionate Scorpio, loving fiercely, turning suddenly—loyal until crossed, then a force to be reckoned with.

Henry and Anne built their relationship on this kind of capricious attraction, full of conversation and temptation, commitments and reversals. They flirted in front of the whole court—where no one knew if this was a kind of courtly love or the beginning of a serious affair. They talked and teased while eating, while dancing, while walking the broad halls of Whitehall, and then, presumably, in darker corners, private rooms, and then, finally, in bed.

Words seduced Henry and Anne before touch took over. Words seduced us as well. Our talk was bolstered by what we read in our classes, and we argued about the influence of Lady Macbeth and the stubborn silence of Hester Prynne; we applied Freudian and feminist theories to the cross-dressing in *Twelfth Night* and Emily Dickinson's poetry and the real-life erotic adventures of Henry Miller and Anaïs Nin. We cast ourselves in the roles of characters, authors, and critics and read our own lives against their plotlines and analyses. The more I read about Henry and Anne's romance, the more I started to hold my life up to hers, to see where the edges overlapped, to see what I might learn from her slow rise and rapid fall.

After three years of marriage and only a daughter to show for it, Henry and Anne's relationship began to founder. One of her waiting women, Jane Seymour, had caught the king's eye, and it was all too easy to make him believe that his marriage to Anne had been a mistake: she was incapable of giving him the heir she had promised; she had committed adultery and even incest to try to conceive a son behind his back; she was a witch, a traitor, a monster; she had ensorcelled him. Her enemies rallied against her, and in the spring of 1536 she was arrested and tried for treason. Three weeks later she was dead.

By the time I left for London, I suspected my days with B were numbered. A young blonde woman, new to the program and already acting as his protégé, seemed all too ready to take my place. The ocean between us was 3,500 miles wide. Long-distance phone calls were few and far between. We were young and uncertain of our future—together or apart. So when the phone rang its foreign pulse in the middle of the night, I picked it up already knowing who it was and fairly sure what he would say.

"I don't want you anymore," B said.

After which I said, with a truth and simplicity that surprised me, "I know."

It was one in the morning London time, and I set the phone gently in its cradle, lay back in my bed, and stared at the ceiling, listening to the vague traffic on Euston Road. And when some internal clock ran out, I turned on my side, pulling the covers with me, and slept.

The next day I toured Hampton Court Palace. What I remember most is the guide dressed as a courtier and how he showed us, at someone's request, his codpiece—even though he said he felt uneasy about wearing one and tried to hide it behind his purse. And then there was the hallway that the guide claimed Katherine Howard, Henry VIII's fifth wife, who actually was guilty of adultery, ran down to beg for mercy from the king, and I thought about how many times I have pleaded for love against the inevitable. There was the gift shop with a silver tray full of little paper cups of mead to sample, and I kept drinking them until I was stumbling around the postcards, the needlepoint pillows, the Henry VIII pencil sharpeners. There were pencils that had a picture of each wife—Catherine of Aragon near the point, Catherine Parr near the eraser—so you could sharpen them away in the order that they were divorced, beheaded, and died. I went back for more mead before I found the watch that showed Henry VIII in the middle of its face, with a second hand shaped like an ax that cut through the pictures of his wives at 1, 3, 5, 7, 9, and 11 o'clock, so every minute all of them would be dispatched. It all seemed so inexorable. I drank a last cup of mead, bought a bottle, bought the watch and the pencil sharpener and some pencils too. Back in my room, I sharpened away Catherine of Aragon and listened to my new watch tick as the phone didn't ring and no one stopped by.

The next day I toured the Tower of London—stopping for a long moment at Traitors' Gate, the way to nearly certain death, where barges took prisoners over the Thames's yellow-gray water. I saw Henry VIII's enormous armor, fifty-seven inches at the chest and fifty-four at the waist, and thought about how he had protected himself against even his own conscience, ordering his wives away days before their divorce or execution, distracting himself through hunting or by spending time with the woman who would become his next wife. I charmed one of the guards into letting me slip behind the altar of the Chapel Royal of St. Peter ad Vincula so I could stand over Anne Boleyn's grave. There was no stone or statue, no sculpture of the queen in repose; there was only a small square slab set in the floor with her name and dates and coat of arms. I tried to feel something but didn't. Instead, I wondered what her corpse looked like now, and if her head was buried separately from her body, wrapped in cloth perhaps, and what it would be like to be beheaded, and if she was still conscious for at least a few moments afterward and, if so, what she thought.

Later that long weekend I walked south to the Thames, crossed Waterloo Bridge, and walked east along the bank to a bench that sat apart from the rest. I sat and watched the tide come in, rising to cover the small rocks and tires at the edge of the riverbed, the watermarks left on stone walls, the dark mosses staining the pilings of each bridge.

A tidal river. How odd. I thought back to the last river I had stood over, the Kennebec in Maine, and how furiously it ran along its banks, how whole trees had coursed through the churning water like monsters, how safe and warm B's arms had felt around me. I thought of the stagnant ochre water outside Traitors' Gate and all the pleading of those doomed to pass through it. I sat watching the Thames rise with the tide, and I knew the tears would come, not now but soon, and that the loss would hit me, not hard, but hard enough to remind me that sometimes, not always, you get nothing. But sometimes nothing is better than forever. Anything is still possible.

Widow Fantasies

There is only one kind of shock worse than the totally unexpected:
the expected for which one has refused to prepare.

Mary Renault

I would like to say that I have prepared for my death, but that's not true. It's not my death that I am secretly preparing for: it's J's. My husband is eleven years older than I am. Sometimes I am jealous of these years, often I am unaware of them, but when I think about our endgame, those eleven years become my enemy.

My friend N's husband is also older than she is. Once she was talking with him about what she would do when she was very old—live in a brownstone in Boston, she said—and her husband stopped her. "Wait a minute," he said. "Where am I in all this?" When N didn't have a quick answer, he accused her: "You've been having widow fantasies!" They laughed it off, but those words have stuck with me.

I met my first widow at a weekend writing conference. Actually, I had known widows before, but I never thought of them as such. My aunt had been a widow since I was a small child, but I always thought of her as simply my aunt. And surely there were other widows— invisible widows—ones who had remarried or ones I assumed had never married. But the widow at Bard College was first and foremost a widow to me—more than a woman, more than a writer. I was wary of her; I kept my distance. I had been with J for a year, and already I knew I would marry him. I also thought that someday I would be his widow.

She looked stricken, her blue eyes had the gleam of pending tears, her short dark hair was sharp and brittle. You could always sense when she entered the room; she seemed untouchable. No one knew what to say to her. What could you say other than *I'm so sorry*? What could you do other than pull your eyebrows in and draw your mouth tight in an effort to show sympathy for something you couldn't even begin to understand?

I don't remember her name, but I am haunted by her blue eyes and the blue waters of Lily Lake. She wrote about trying to swim across Lily Lake as a child and how she could only reach the floating dock in the middle. "Hard and easy were irrelevant," she wrote. "What lay on the other shore?" We all felt the metaphor.

In the crypt of the National Cathedral, just off the Resurrection Chapel, is a dark alcove illuminated only by candles lit in prayer. It's the smallest, darkest, most private place in the cathedral—the best place for grief. This is where I'll come, I thought. Early in the day only a few candles are lit; by evening the candles blaze with light. I sit and watch them for a while. One burns out, and it seems as if the plume of smoke that rises when the flame dies is a culmination of the prayer that lit the candle in the first place. It is one last effort to get to God. It is beautiful.

Once a woman was in this chapel, her eyes swollen and her mouth tight, and I made a wide circle around her. I kept coming back, though, wanting to sit in the chapel myself. But she was there for longer than I would wait. Was she a widow too?

In the Middle Ages a woman—a widow—of exceptional spiritual depth might become an anchoress. An anchoress might live in a solitary cell attached to a church. One window would look into the church so she could worship, but the other would look out into the street so that people could come and seek counsel. In Russia a devout man or a woman might have lived as a *poustinik*, living alone but not in isolation, always ready to welcome and serve a stranger. The Russian word for *solitude* means "being with everybody."

When I learned this, I thought, *Maybe this is what I will do*. I had always thought that if J died first and we had no children, I'd throw myself into humanitarian work, however dangerous. Without J, I wouldn't necessarily want to live, so why not do all the good I could until I died? I was reminded of this while watching the end of *The Constant Gardener*, when Ralph Fiennes's character travels to the spot where his wife was killed to wait for his own death. How hard those last few hours must have been, waiting and remembering, his mind prepared to face something the body fights against until the last possible moment.

When J and I were not yet engaged, I had a fender bender, and J drove me to pick up my car from the shop. The night was windy and wet, but as I followed him home, his taillights shone steady in the rainy dark. Halfway there we heard sirens, and then we passed an accident. A woman had run off the road and into a tree, her face a pale flash of fear as we passed. I took a breath, tightened my grip on the steering wheel, and followed J's taillights. And then I thought, *This is what death will be like*. It will be a dark rainy night that I will follow him through until we cross into that undiscovered country from which no traveler returns.

Has any of this prepared me for the expected shock of widowhood? We think of fantasies as daydreams about our desires, but the word *fantasy* comes from the Greek φαντασία, literally "a making visible." When my friend N fantasized about a future without her husband, was she daydreaming a desire, or was she simply "making visible" the road ahead? And when I have thought, in dim chapels and dark movie theaters, about a future without J, am I making the possible— the probable—visible? Or am I seeing my fears, projected ghosts of what frightens me the most?

Joan Didion, in *The Year of Magical Thinking*, says that "grief turns out to be a place none of us know until we reach it." Like the widow I knew for a weekend and then only from a distance. Like swimming across Lily Lake to the floating dock, looking to the other shore and wondering, Who lives there? "Hard and easy are irrelevant," the widow wrote, and I knew she was no longer talking about swimming.

Striking

(There are twenty matches in a book.)

1.

A prickle. A glimmer. A shiver of feeling. A moment ago you were alone with your thoughts. Things were clear, straightforward. But now you are haunted.

2.

Haunt: to materialize, appear in, frequent, visit, disturb, torment. None of these captures the contrary nature of hauntedness—to be filled with hollowness, to ache for something not entirely wanted, to have and have not.

3.

I read *Wuthering Heights* over the course of two gray days in January. Afterward I walked across a frozen field to the woods. The grass was stiff and pale, the color of lichen, and the woods were very quiet. I actually whispered, Heathcliff? No reply. But by *Heathcliff* I meant, of course, someone else.

4.

I was away from my family. I had steeped myself in Cathy and Heathcliff's story as if in a hot bath. But I stayed too long, until I became chilled, until the last line about the unquiet slumbers in that quiet earth released me into the still winter air, the silent woods.

5.

Was I trying to haunt myself?

6.

I once wrote about being balanced on that fine point between forever and nothing, where a breath of feeling would push me to one or the other. But here there was no current to guide me, no wind to sail against, no breath but my own clouding faintly in the air.

7.

There, at the edge of the woods, the cold bled into my lungs, seeped through my soles, crept beneath my clothes. The book lay closed and far away. Whatever I was conjuring slumbered on.

8.

We can't control when the ghost materializes or what drives it away. Sometimes it's a presence, more often an absence. "Let me in," says the voice at the window, "I'm come home."

9.

The voice at my window says *wait*, says *no*, says *quiet*, is quiet. I strain to hear a wish for home.

10.

The tension between not being let in and not being let go fixes us. Especially when it's the not-being-let-in that won't let you go. You're held at the threshold. You're turned away, but you can't turn away.

11.

I want to turn away.

12.

Cathy says: "I *am* Heathcliff! He's always, always in my mind: not as a pleasure . . . but as my own being." She says that her love for her husband "is like the foliage in the woods: time will change it . . . as winter changes the trees," but her "love for Heathcliff resembles the eternal rocks beneath: a source of little visible delight, but necessary."

13.

Have my own past loves been merely leaves on the trees? Why am I standing in these cold woods, away from my eternal rock, whispering the name of someone else?

14.

Strike a match and watch it burn. Strike a blow and crush the match. Strike a chord and burn with loss. Strike a deal and turn away.

15.

When Heathcliff and Cathy are apart, "the gunpowder lay as harmless as sand, because no fire came near to explode it." But after Heathcliff returns, the weather cools, the leaves fall, and the powder explodes. Then Heathcliff is left only with sand. Without Cathy the fire won't catch. He is alone in a desert of his own making.

16.

And here I am, lighting matches, trying to see what they illuminate, tossing them away before they gutter out, uncertain whether they'll fall on powder or sand.

17.

Here I am at the edge of the woods, remembering all the diverging roads I took to stand here.

18.

Here I am haunted by my need to be haunted, by my reluctance to let anything stay buried, by my desire to bring hauntedness itself into this weak winter light and see it truly for what it is.

19.

At the end of *Wuthering Heights* three graves lie at the edge of the moor. What am I at the edge of? Who will I lie beside, and who will lie between us? Or am I to be the one between?

20.

That night I drive home in the dark. The road swells over hills, my headlights showing only what lies immediately ahead. "Be with me always," I think of the things that haunt me, the love of my young life, the places now lost, the mistakes I have made, and the mysteries I will never solve. Outside my moving car are shadowed yards and black fields, houses with dark windows or only one upstairs light on. Most of the living I pass are sleeping. And the dead—who can say?

I'm driving home to those I hold dear, but I'm not there yet.

V

On Looking

On Looking

We are looking at a Siberian camel. It is lying on top of its folded legs, long-lashed eyes blinking slowly, wobbly lips frosted with green, contentedly chewing its cud.

"Look at her eyelashes," a woman says to her friend. "She doesn't need mascara."

"Look at his lips," a man says with faint disgust.

The camel lumbers to its feet and sways gently. Its expression doesn't change, and it doesn't look away as—

"It's pooping!" a boy yells. "Look at its poop!"

The camel strolls along the fence, moving toward a woman who calls to it. "That's it. Come to me. Come to me," she croons. The camel stops near her, murmurs its lips over a few strands of hay, swings its head to look at some unknown movement, some object of interest only to camels.

"He knows, he knows," the woman chants. "He walks with the people."

In the museum it is much more quiet. The rooms are high ceilinged, the floors bare, the light cool and controlled. So are the people, mostly.

I stop in front of Domenichino's *The Rebuke of Adam and Eve* and look. Adam is half-shrugging, half-gesturing to a cringing Eve, while God swoops down to them, reclining on a couch of angels, a red silk canopy flaring above him.

"Driving them out of the garden," a middle-aged woman narrates to her friend.

The friend plays God: "Get out. You screwed up—now get out." They laugh and move on, their hard heels echoing on the bare floor.

A man looks for a moment, pauses, says: "Adam's like, 'I don't know. Don't look at me—look at her.'" Another brief laugh.

A child reads the title out loud: "*The Rebuke of Adam and Eve.* Mom, what's *rebuke?*"

When the model walks in the classroom, we are all disappointed. Too old, too fat, and—for half the class this too is a disappointment— male. His thinning blond hair is pulled back in a ponytail, and a thick handlebar goatee obscures his mouth. He has crow's-feet and sloping shoulders, and his deeply cut tank top shows the curve of his hanging stomach. When he shakes hands with the teacher and leaves to change, I imagine him either riding a Harley-Davidson or sweeping a metal detector over a beach.

The other students, most of them barely in their twenties, all of them at least ten years younger than I am, exchange glances. I look down at my block of clay.

When the model returns, he is wearing a thin teal terry cloth robe and black plastic flip-flops. He climbs onto the turntable in the center of the room, adjusts a cushion, and sits on a wooden cube.

He shrugs out of the robe, which drops to the floor.

The room is silent.

"Mouna is not a shy woman," the presenter says. "But she is not used to standing up in front of a crowd and being looked at." I am in the crowd at the Adornment Pavilion at the Smithsonian Folklife Festival looking at Mouna. Mouna stands onstage, not used to being looked at.

When prompted, Mouna holds out her palms so that we can see the henna designs intricately stained into her skin. When asked, she lifts the hem of her robe so we can see the cuffs of her trousers, embroidered with ornate silver vines. When instructed, we look at her elaborate makeup, the kohl lining her eyes and extending her eyebrows so that they almost meet over her nose, the bright lipstick, the harsh lines of blush. But her eyes remain aloof, her gaze skimming over the tops of our heads, never meeting our own.

He walks with the people? No. This camel hasn't walked with the people for years—possibly for his whole life. He walks separately from the people, not with them, not alongside them—as he might have in the deserts of Siberia. Instead, a waist-high fence and a camel-deep pit keep us apart—but so does our gaze and our speech. We contain this camel—as well as all the other animals at the zoo—with words, narrating each and every action: "It's looking at you . . . It's getting up . . . It's pooping!" Our words walk with the camel. It can do nothing without our commentary.

Later in the museum I walk into a room of Van Goghs and overhear the typical docent's speech: "You can see he had a different worldview from the impressionists. Notice the brushstrokes . . . notice his use of color." Notice his missing ear, I silently add.

But then I notice the word *notice*. At the zoo there was only looking at things—no "Notice that big pile of poop!" or "Notice how fat that hippo is." The expert instructs us to notice, but the people who walk through museums look. In the medieval wing: "Look at their floppy hats!" Of a painting of a painter painting: "Look—he's painting it. Hey, look at that; that's pretty good."

Paintings are made to be looked at. They have no life outside of our gaze; we animate them with our words.

When the model's robe hits the floor, he is facing away from me. All I can see is his back, an expanse of rusty body hair, the points of his elbows, and his surprisingly compact behind that almost disappears as he sits on it. But I can also see the faces across the room, the wide eyes flicking immediately to his midsection, looking first at what is usually seen last.

Every five minutes he rotates a quarter-turn, and ten minutes into the session I am faced with his bristly chest, his hanging stomach, and what sits immediately beneath it—his enormous penis.

I blink and look away, at his arm, at the clay arm I pretend to work on. I don't want the people across the room to assess my face the way I had assessed theirs, but most of all I don't want to blush. But God it's huge. It lies like a sultan on a fleshy satin cushion, and as the afternoon passes, it relaxes and—unbelievably—uncoils further.

Break is called, the model puts on his robe and his flip-flops, and the class flees to the hall and the steps outside. There, in clusters of two and three, they whisper; those who are alone pull out their cell phones. All look furtively back at the art room as they describe the naked body of the man they have been looking at for the last half-hour, their tones ranging from scorn to fascination.

I hold myself apart from these conversations, keeping my words to myself. I don't want to talk about what I have seen—especially with strangers. I don't want to feel like I have to talk about it. It was a naked man. No more, no less. But later that day, during a longer break, when the rest of the students leave to buy a sandwich or a cup of coffee, I pull out my cell phone and make my own call.

Mouna's gaze does not meet ours, but why should it? When the presenter speaks in English, all Mouna hears are sounds, punctuated occasionally by her own name. After awhile she stops responding to her name, trusting that "—— Mouna —— Mouna's —— " is as benign as "As a woman from the southern part of Oman, Mouna wears a such-and-such head scarf. You can also tell from the embroidery on Mouna's sleeves that she is from Salalah."

The Folklife Festival is in Washington DC, and people from all over the country are there. We make quiet comments to our friends and family—"Look at that embroidery," "Look at her bracelets," "It must be hot under all that"—until the time comes to ask questions.

"Do you have to cover your head?" Yes, the presenter says. If you leave your house without covering your head, it's like you're not fully dressed. "Don't you find that restrictive?" No. It's what we do.

"How do you clean your clothes?" We wash them, the presenter says. "Do you use washing machines?" Yes—if it's cotton. If it's silk, we get it dry-cleaned. "Dry-cleaned! You have dry cleaners—the same kind we have?" Yes. A smile.

"Are there meanings behind the patterns?" No, she says. We just like the way they look. "Really? I find that hard to believe." Really. Another smile.

Having visited the Adornment Pavilion before, many of these questions sound dumb to my now educated ears, but I remember wanting to know the same kinds of things on my first visit. I had been afraid to ask. Now, though, I start wondering what these Omani women think of American women who are amazed that they have washing machines and insist that each pattern on their clothing has meaning. The stitching on the back pockets of my jeans doesn't have meaning, nor do the stripes on my T-shirt. What are we looking for through these questions? And what do the Omani women hear in them? What do they see?

Is the Siberian camel looking at you? I want to ask the crooning woman. Or only at a shape that's making foreign sounds and meaningless gestures?

I leave the camel and go to the Ape House. A small tribe of gorillas is on display. One paces in front of the glass, one picks through a pile of fruit and grasses, one has its back to us, and one sits removed from the rest, high up on a rock outcropping—a female with rich brown eyes. My gaze meets that of the sitter. I think we are really looking at each other. I *want* us to be really looking at each other. I want her to see that I am different from the other people here: the boy pounding on the glass (despite the sign that says not to); the woman who grimaces and says, "It stinks in here"; the teenager who laughs, pointing,

"Look at its tits!" I want her to see sympathy and understanding in my eyes, that we are two primates separated by only a few twists of a chromosome—and a wall of shit-splattered Plexiglas.

The gorilla's gaze shifts an inch to a spot just above my ear—a spot she stares at just as intently, just as soulfully—and I know that to her I am no different from any other moving sound-making shape on this side of the glass.

In the museum Rembrandt looks back at me. Not when he is a young man but in his *Self-Portrait 1659*. It is as if he is trying to communicate over three hundred years and three thousand miles. The painting is dark, with rich hues of brown in his clothing and his eyes, a slightly duller brown for the background. From these dark surroundings emerges his face, framed by twin clouds of silver hair and a faint goatee under his shadowed mouth. But all of this acts as another frame—a frame for his eyes, which shine out of all this darkness with a pained warmth. I can feel the weight of his stare, the weight of experience behind his stare, and I feel that he is trying to tell me something, even if I'm not quite sure what it is he is trying to say.

But Rembrandt's gaze is not a separate gaze, like that of the camel or the gorilla. Those gazes are independent from mine—even if they pass over me with indifference. The gaze of the art is reflective, as the gaze of animals has become. Art shows me back to myself—and me to you, and you to me.

Do you laugh at *Adam and Eve Rebuked*? Do you play God? Or do you stand back silently, listening to others talk, saving bits of what you hear to mull over later?

When you stand in front of Rembrandt, what does he tell you?

Whatever you read in his gaze, like the gorilla, he'll look at the next person to walk by his frame—the bored teenager, the struggling art student, the recent widow—in exactly the same way.

Does the model ever look back at me? Yes.

Occasionally I meet his eyes when he is on the turntable, usually when I am working on his head or face, sometimes (disproportionately often, it seems to me) when I am working on rolling a bit of clay into a penis or flattening a ball of clay, like a jelly donut, to rest it on. Whenever our eyes meet, we both quickly flick our gaze away.

On break we all stalk the halls of the art building or sit outside, stretching, in the sun. During these breaks the model often eats Goya Chocolate Wafers and I try to fit this detail into the lives I imagine for him—the Harley rider, the beachcomber—but without success. An unseen boundary seems to separate him—the one who has been naked—from the rest of us, protected by our clothes. When our eyes meet outside the classroom, I quickly drop my gaze, duck my head, and pull the corners of my mouth into that flat, tight-lipped smile that never fools anyone. I know how it must look. I don't want to appear cold, distant, uncomfortable—but I am. I want to keep that distance between us more than I feel the social need to connect.

Back in the classroom, his nakedness begins to lose its allure. We are busy trying to replicate his shape in clay, and it matters less and less what his shape actually is. The teacher points and says, "See the line of his shoulder" or "See how his calf muscle curves" or "See the angle of his knee." That I can do; I can see his shape and understand how it can be reflected in my own sculpture. But I cannot find a way to see the person who inhabits those lines and curves and angles. In the classroom or outside, naked or clothed, I cannot do it.

Mouna never looks at me. When she is on display in the Adornment Pavilion, she doesn't look at the crowd there but above our heads, toward the crowd outside. It is hard to tell if she is looking at anything or only standing in suspension, waiting to be released from the presenter's droning, her incomprehensible spell.

Later I see Mouna dancing as part of the Al Majd Ensemble, a traditional dance troupe from southern Oman. Immediately I notice that she only really looks at the other female dancers. In fact, all the female dancers only look at each other. The male dancers prance and whirl around them, smiling with bright eyes, inviting them closer with a soft word or a swoop of the head, but the women stay nearly immobile, each waving a corner of her robe at hip height, eyes fixed to the floor or deliberately staring into the middle distance. Is this part of the dance? Or part of the culture? I don't know. There is more than the language barrier between us.

When the presenter had asked Mouna to show her hands, her cuffs, her makeup, she used the phrase "You can see—" This invited me to look, but it also implied a hope of engagement, that some kind of exchange would pass between us, the observer and the observed. I could physically see the henna on her hands, but with the presenter's help I could also see how and why it was applied. Watching the dancing, I can see the motions and gestures, but I can't see the motives behind them. I am on my own.

But of all the Omani women I see, the image that stays with me is one of a masked Bedouin woman. I can look at her—her black robes and her busy hands, a dark velvet mask covering her nose and upper lip—but through this mask I can't see how she looks back at me. I can see her eyes clearly but nothing else—no expression, no gesture, no words.

I know that she is looking out at the world and at me in it, but I can only guess at her thoughts. She might be looking at my bare arms the way I would look at a woman's nipple peeping out of a bikini top. She might see my cropped hair as a punishment, a rejection of womanhood, a sign of mourning, a mark of liberation. She might think of my freedom with envy or distrust or pity. Or does she look at me with a more reflective curiosity, as I look at her?

I have no way of knowing what is behind her mask, any more than she knows what is behind my bare face. We are two people with nothing between us but distance, a distance bridged only by looking, being looked at, and trying still harder to see.

The Ownership of Memory

She was gorgeous. Her white skin emerged from her velvet dress like pale petals from a dark stem. Her hair was brown and rich, curled and piled, and secured with a pearl pin. But there was something in her expression that made me stop and sit and stare. She didn't meet my gaze but looked off to the right, over my shoulder and to the far corner of the room. Her eyebrows were thoughtful—or wary. She might be sensitive or skittish, dignified or tentative. She was *Mrs. Charles E. Inches (Louise Pomeroy)*, a portrait by John Singer Sargent.

I sat on a bench in the Boston Museum of Fine Art, thinking that I'd look at Mrs. Charles E. Inches for a long time. I had read Jeannette Winterson's essay "Art Objects" and was envious that she could look at a painting for a full hour—despite all the different thoughts that press into her mind, threatening to evict the art itself.

I wanted to look at Mrs. Inches for an hour but soon discovered that I couldn't look at her for more than a minute—not because of impatience or boredom, or because I got distracted wondering how I might look in her red velvet dress, but because I felt an overwhelming desire to own her. I left the bench and hit the gift shop. There I found her in a bay of postcards, and for only a dollar I bought her.

When I returned to the room of Sargents, my Mrs. Inches stayed in my bag, but I noticed that the painting was brighter—her skin creamier, her eyes more alive, her dress a more vibrant red. I knew the card was a poor imitation, and I felt it was wrong to want the card, to need the card, before I could allow myself to really look at the original, but I pretended I didn't care. With my bag on the bench beside me, I looked at Mrs. Inches for the half-hour I had left and then went to meet friends in the city.

Later that evening, during the long bus ride home, I pulled the card from my bag. In *Ways of Seeing* John Berger writes, "If you buy a painting you also buy the look of the thing it represents." He writes this in order to explain the art I usually skip on museum visits—the lavish tables spread with glistening oysters and ruddy fruits, the limp dead pheasant guarded by the loyal hunting dog, the glossy cow that placidly stands tied to a tree on Lord So-and-So's estate. I can understand this kind of ownership, the need to own displays of wealth, but it was hard for me to apply this to my own need. I certainly didn't want to own Mrs. Charles E. Inches the person, but I could see how I coveted the look of the things she represented—wealth, beauty, sensitivity, dignity. But I didn't need her or her image to remind me of these desires.

I had sat on the bench; she had hung on the wall. Both of us were silent and still. There were others in the room, but if they spoke, it was barely above a whisper. Occasionally someone would walk between us—a flicker of shadow. Time passed strangely. It was only a minute before I retreated from the immediacy of the painting to what was familiar and distant—the gift shop, the transaction of purchase, the postcard.

Only on the bus ride home did I think of John Berger. "When the camera reproduces a painting, it destroys the uniqueness of its image. As a result its meaning changes." This, I think, was the root of my unease at needing to buy this postcard. I don't like the thought that a reproduction of this unique object can be bought with pocket change, carried out of the museum, travel four hundred miles, and be pinned to the bulletin board above my desk in Washington. But at the same time I want it. I want to own it, to gaze at it at my convenience— without driving for eight hours or flying for however many dollars. I want a physical, tangible reminder of what I saw and a visual trigger for what I felt when I saw it.

I knew all this in the minute I first looked at Mrs. Inches, even if I couldn't yet admit it. Once I had the postcard, my future with her was assured. I was free to look at her in the present, for as much time as I then had.

Three months later I was walking through a cornfield in search of a cemetery in the middle of Virginia. A fox trotted across the path in front of me and disappeared in the forest of stalks with barely a rustle. I was searching for Stonewall Jackson's lost arm.

Stonewall Jackson, a general in the Confederate army, was a fanatical Presbyterian and a hypochondriac who sucked on lemons for their taste but avoided black pepper for his health. He was fearless in the face of death and received his nickname for standing "like a stone wall" against an onslaught of Union gunfire at First Manassas. But one May night in 1863, after a victory over Hooker's forces, Jackson took advantage of the darkness to scout ahead of his own line. When he returned, a group of North Carolina pickets mistook him for the enemy and opened fire. Four of Jackson's men were killed, and three bullets lodged in his left arm. Later that night the arm was amputated; the next day it was buried.

In Chancellorsville, 150 years later, the story of this arm is surprisingly well documented. A large quartz boulder marks the place where Jackson fell, and signs along Route 3 mark the "Wounding of Jackson" and "Jackson's Amputation." But the cemetery in which the arm was buried was not marked. I knew that an aide had taken the arm to his own family graveyard, and I learned from one of the markers that the cemetery was called Ellwood, but I didn't know where it was—only that it was nearby.

I drove through Chancellorsville National Military Park with my eyes open for anything that looked like it might lead to a cemetery. Late in the day, in a gray misty rain, having already given up, I pulled into a driveway to turn around and stopped short at a rusty iron gate with the soldered block letters E L L W O O D.

I hesitated. It was clearly a locked gate, but a faint trail led around it and continued through dense woods. While I didn't want to trespass, I didn't want to retreat either. The mystery of the arm was too great; I left the car in the driveway.

The dark woods increased my sense of unease but also my curiosity. I didn't know if I was heading toward the cemetery or the twin barrels of a shotgun, but I walked until the trees gave way to a clearing. An abandoned barn leaned into a surrounding cornfield. Two vultures eyed me from its sagging roof, but I kept going. I wanted to find the arm.

I had deliberately not brought a camera but instead brought a notebook and a pen. I had been so intrigued with reading about the Civil War that I wanted to experience it closer to the way the soldiers had experienced it. I didn't want to walk from DC to Chancellorsville barefoot or wear a wool uniform in August. I didn't want to suffer from slow starvation or crab apple–induced dysentery, festering wounds, or the sepsis of a war-torn mind—but I wanted to see and record the way the soldiers did.

A small sign pointed to a path through some boxwoods and then cornstalks. Although I could hear an occasional car in the distance, it felt like I had stepped back in time. The stalks rustled, and the mist beaded in my hair, and a red fox trotted across the path.

Alone, I continued, heart beating faster than my footsteps, wondering what else the cornfield held. But then, just ahead, was another clearing, and under a lone tree, encircled by a knee-high iron fence, was the graveyard. Among the nubs of worn stone marking the family graves was another stone, only slightly taller, engraved with "Arm of Stonewall Jackson May 3 1863."

The place was eerie, but I was starting to appreciate its otherness— the suspicious vultures on the roof of the barn, the reassuring drone of the crickets filling what would have been an uncanny silence, the fox, the tree, the stone. It was hard to imagine this as a battle site with one hundred thousand men fighting, many dying. It was hard to imagine the aide with his box and his shovel, standing on this same spot, about to do his last duty to the arm of his commander. It was hard to imagine the arm, now a bone, nestled in its box under the earth. And how it had once been attached to a man who had taught philosophy at the Virginia Military Institute, married a minister's daughter, fathered a baby girl, and after leading his division of the Army of Northern Virginia through some of the war's most decisive battles, finally died of pneumonia in a small weathered cottage a week after the amputation.

But I did imagine those things because I had little other choice. There was nothing to distract me—no camera to limit what I was seeing, no viewfinder through which to frame the grave, no need to stalk it from different angles to find the best shot. There was no National Park shop in this field, ready to sell me postcards and books, authentic Civil War minié balls or fake Confederate dollars. There was nothing between me and what I was looking at.

The graveyard was silent and still, aside from the crickets and the breeze through the grass. The mist blurred the boundaries of the woods and the fields, and I felt the distance in time closing— the distance between the burial of this arm and my looking at its gravestone—and I knew I wouldn't need anything else to remember this moment.

The Island of Topaz

My grandmother's rings lay jumbled together in a small vinyl pouch, which she had hidden under a stack of newspapers at the bottom of her laundry hamper. The summer before my wedding my father gave them to me. Sitting in my apartment, I pour them out onto a plain white plate. I stir the pile with my finger.

The Oval Topaz

My grandmother's sister, my great-aunt Win, had been a combat nurse during World War II and was stationed in England and France. One day she borrowed a jeep, sussed out my Uncle Norman, a pilot for the RAF, and went shopping on the black market. There she bought this animal-eyed ring for her sister in Bloomfield, New Jersey—the topaz the size and shape of my grandmother's smallest fingernail, the gold setting around it thick and plain.

According to *The Curious Lore of Precious Stones*, Pliny claimed that topaz came from an island in the Red Sea called Topazos, whose name comes from the word *topazein*, "to conjecture," because this fogbound island was so difficult to find.

Where had this ring come from? Who had owned it? Was it my imagination, or did I see the shadow of an inscription long since buffed away? What would this ring say if it could? Perhaps I don't want to know.

I remember this topaz ring on my grandmother's pinkie nearly every day, the pinkie she held high while drinking a cup of tea after dinner or while carefully placing a Scrabble tile or while drawing a card from a well-shuffled deck.

The Big Amethyst

According to mythology, the Greek god Dionysus, thrown into a rage by a perceived insult from a nameless mortal, ordered a group of tigers to attack the next person who crossed his path. Enter Amethystos, a young maiden on her way to worship at the shrine of Artemis, virgin goddess of the hunt and of the moon. When the tigers sprang at her, Amethystos prayed to the goddess, and Artemis saved her by transforming her into a pillar of white stone. Dionysus, seeing what he had caused, wept and poured a libation of wine over the stone in apology. The white quartz was dyed purple, and the gem we know as amethyst was born.

According to the thirteenth-century *Book of Wings*, if you carve a bear onto an amethyst, it can put demons to flight. Wearing an amethyst could also induce dreams. But its most common usage was to ward off drunkenness. The Greek word *amethystos* can be translated as "not drunk."

My grandmother's amethyst ring is enormous, larger than one of the dice in our Yahtzee game. It fit her then-chubby hand with surprising grace. Even if she didn't know the mythological origins of amethyst or its supposed properties, my grandmother needed its protection.

Her father had been a hard-drinking man. Admiral William Frederick "Bull" Halsey once sent my great-grandfather Alexander MacLennan a photograph of himself, the admiral, sitting on a horse. The inscription reads: "It looks like I've had more scotch than you, Mac—but that's not possible."

I don't know that I ever saw my grandmother drunk, but cocktail hour was a ritual for my grandparents. My grandfather would take the bus home from work in Manhattan. He'd get off at Broad Street and Mountain Avenue and walk home. As soon as he got in the door, he made a drink—Dewar's White Label on the rocks with a splash. My grandmother joined him with a Canadian Club and a splash. That's how their evenings began.

The same drinks, served at the same time and with the same anchoring dish of nuts or cheese curls, all before moving smoothly to the dinner table. Perhaps this sedate adult ritual tamed what had once been so wild in her childhood.

But the stone in my grandmother's ring, even if it did help ward off drunkenness, did not come from a transformed virgin in ancient Greece but from a mine in modern Brazil, where some of the largest geode-containing amethysts can be found. They also come from Canada, where my grandmother spent her childhood. If you're from North America, amethyst is the birthstone for the month of February. Saint Valentine is said to have worn an amethyst ring engraved with a cupid. This sounds out of character for a saint, but many leaders of the Roman Catholic Church wear amethyst rings as part of their office. Amethysts have long been considered a symbol of divine understanding and spiritual exploration.

I don't remember ever having a conversation with my grandmother about divine understanding and spiritual exploration. I knew she went to church nearly every Sunday morning. She had been raised a Catholic by her mother, an English Catholic, but by the time she grew up, she hated them. Her Scottish father wouldn't have been too keen on Catholics either, even though he married one. In Scotland they had egged the pope, and when my great-grandmother died, my grandmother's Catholicism was buried with her.

My grandmother watched early morning televangelists, fascinated. She watched all kinds of trials—the McCarthy hearings, the House Un-American Activities Committee hearings, the Eichmann trial, the Patty Hearst trial, the O.J. Simpson trial. She watched tennis obsessively, even though she never played, and boxing, even though she hated violence. My grandmother was an odd mix, like Artemis, the goddess of both hunting and chastity, purity and blood sport.

Greek gods—particularly Artemis—had a habit of answering cries for help with inhuman transformations (Amethystos turned into stone, Daphne into a tree, Taygete into a doe). If my grandmother had asked to be protected, she would have prayed to the Father, Son, or Holy Ghost. But if Artemis, long-neglected goddess of the hunt and of the moon, had chanced to overhear, she might have granted my grandmother's prayer in her usual backhanded way, perhaps with something the moon was thought to cause: lunacy.

The Three Aquamarines

The name *aquamarine* means "seawater."

A Greek lapidary from the third or fourth century instructed sailors to wear an amulet of aquamarine to ensure safe passage. Some sailors believed mermaids' tails were made of aquamarine. Others slipped an aquamarine under their pillows so that they would sleep well through the night.

Grandma had three aquamarine rings—the big one, the small one, and the one with three square stones set straight across. The way I thought of them in a group reminded me of the way I thought about Columbus's ships: the *Niña*, the *Pinta*, and the *Santa Maria*. The big one is so pale it almost looks clear; it is the size of one of the Chiclets my grandmother used to carry in her purse. The small one is a deeper blue, and the three set straight across are the deepest blue of all. She wore these rings at different times but nearly always on her right ring finger.

Aquamarine is the birthstone for March: "In like a lion, out like a lamb." I don't know how my grandmother came into this world. I can imagine her being born fat and pink with a mop of dark hair, blue eyes shut tight, her fresh lungs a set of bellows to pump out her screams. This would have been while her mother was still alive, before she knew her father was a tyrant. I can imagine her as a toddler, stumping around on wobbly legs, grabbing with sticky fingers, screeching like a little cub when she didn't get her way. But now she is lost in the gauzy world of dementia.

The Gulf of Mexico is only 20 miles away from their retirement community in Florida, which I only visited once ("No children" was one of the rules, which left me deeply offended). The Atlantic Ocean, on the other side of the state, is 120 miles away. But my grandparents rarely went there. Instead, they lived with a swimming pool and the water hazards of the golf course. But even these could not be fully domesticated. CAUTION: HIDDEN DANGER, the signs on the fairways warned; alligators lounged just below the surface of these little ponds, their knobby eyes the only subtle signs of their existence. Sometimes an alligator would brave the sting of chlorine and slide noiselessly into a swimming pool.

Aquamarines may grant a good night's sleep, but dream dictionaries claim that to dream of alligators is to dream of ghostly secrets, lurking threats, hidden dangers. This kind of dream confronts what Jung calls the "Shadow," that dark part of ourselves that is only glimpsed in sudden lunges from the depths. But what of my grandmother? Did she dream at all? Or did her dementia clear her mind of all its shadows and leave it as simple and vacant as a plain white box?

The Round Red Garnet

Garnet comes in many shades of rose, green, and amber, although the color we associate with garnet is a dark, rich red. This is called "pyrope," and its name comes from the Greek *pyropos*, meaning "fiery."

According to *The Curious Lore of Precious Stones*, garnet is a powerful stone. If you carved a lion on a garnet, it would keep you in good health, cure you of disease, restore your honor, and guard you on your travels. Because of its bloodred color, it was thought to cure hemorrhages. Some Asiatic tribes used garnets as bullets, believing that a blood-colored stone would inflict a more deadly wound. In 1892 they were used against British troops on the Kashmir frontier.

My grandmother's garnet is smaller than a bullet. It is the size of a match tip and set high in its gold setting, so that light shines through from the sides and sets its red color ablaze. Two tiny diamonds flank the stone like Phobos and Deimos, the two moons that orbit Mars.

Inside the ring, at its bottom curve, a strip of gold has been added to resize it, perhaps when my grandmother started losing weight and her hands lost their plumpness.

Garnet is the birthstone for January, a month of new years and fresh starts. One year, when my father was nine and his younger sister six, my grandmother made a resolution. "There must be more to life than diapers and detergent," she said, and went to work teaching second grade. My grandfather didn't like this very much. A man of his time was expected to provide for his family; if his wife worked, it was because she had to—not because she wanted to. But my grandmother had some fire in her and wore him down. (I'm sure she didn't know that industrial-grade garnet is often used in sandblasters.)

I was happy to find this smallish red stone among the jumble of her rings. I wanted something that I could wear, something that would bind me to the grandmother I had spent twenty summers with but never really knew. I liked the deep burgundy tones of garnet, even though I never wore gold. At one point I thought I might have the ring reset into silver, but that didn't feel right. The summer before my wedding, my grandmother is still alive. These are still her rings. I'm just their custodian.

Onyx

Onyx is an ominous stone. Its Arabic name is *el jaza*, which means "sadness." Nyx is the Greek goddess of night, and onyx is associated with midnight. Some sources say that onyx brings comfort to the grieving, but more claim that anyone who wears it is subject to fearful dreams, doubts, apprehensions, and, ultimately, loss of capacity. Among the children of the goddess Nyx are Eris (Strife), Geras (Old Age), Ker, and Keres (the Fates of Death).

Onyx is found all over the world. So is the misery it is said to cause. I don't remember my grandmother wearing this ring at all. But I wonder if, after my grandfather died, she turned to it. She would not have known about its supposed properties, but I wonder if she slipped it on her finger instinctively, if only to match the black of her funeral dress, and then fell under its dark power. It was only after my grandfather died that we realized her fears and doubts were symptoms of her loss of capacity, and that without my grandfather's protection she was helpless in the world, and soon would withdraw from it completely.

Her Diamond Engagement Ring and Gold Wedding Band

Diamonds are luminous stones, the gem of noontime and of the sun, the opposite of Onyx's dark omens. They are the hardest known natural minerals, formed deep underground—fifty miles or more—at high temperatures and under tremendous pressure. They are pure carbon, "the building block of life," heated and pressed into crystals that hide until they are washed up by rivers or mined from the depths.

My grandfather first saw my grandmother at Newark State Teachers College, where they both took classes. He saw her doing water ballet in the college pool. I can only imagine what led him to pick her out of that lineup. Did she have a particular grace that stood out against the rest of the rubber-capped girls treading water upside down, one foot pointed out of the water and into the air? Did she paint her toenails red? Was it her small frame, her bright blue eyes, her smile of closely set teeth? Whatever it was, it led him, through a series of dates, to a proposal and to marriage.

The use of diamonds for engagement rings can be traced back through the Middle Ages to the Romans. Diamonds were thought to have the ability to maintain harmony between a husband and wife; they would dim if a spouse was unfaithful. Many believed that diamond deposits were guarded by serpents and used birds of prey to retrieve them. Some thought that they originated from lightning strikes, and others thought they could breed on their own.

My grandmother had worn these two rings for as long as I had known her. I never asked to try them on, the way I asked my mother if I could try on her wedding and engagement rings. My grandmother's rings were embedded in the flesh of her finger. They were the nearly invisible mark of a long-married woman, something I took so much for granted that I didn't even notice them—until I poured her vinyl pouch of rings out onto a white porcelain plate and they fell out too.

Pliny wrote that wearing a diamond wards off insanity, and I wondered how her engagement ring left her finger. Did she slip it off herself and drop it into the vinyl pouch, which she then hid in the bottom of the hamper? Or did a nurse take it from her finger and put it in a Ziploc bag of personal effects? Did my grandmother have any sense of what she lost or what was taken from her? My rational mind knew it was better this way. If left on her hand, these rings could have been lost or stolen. But the thought of my grandmother's bare hand, lying forgotten in her lap or on the arm of a chair or the sheet of a bed, without a reminder of her husband or a talisman to protect her against insanity, pains me.

The diamond is the birthstone of April, the month of Passover, Easter, and spring. Who knows what she's been spared, or what she might become on her release?

The Odd Blue Stone Ring

I can only speculate about this ring. That it has a story, I am sure. But I never saw my grandmother wear it. I never knew it existed until it tumbled out of its pouch with its siblings.

The round blue stone is the same color as a deep summer sky and is cut so that an eight-pointed star shines subtly from its top. It is surrounded by a ring of thirteen clear white stones posing as diamonds, but three of them are missing, the prongs that once held them in place torn away. The surface of the blue stone is dull and scratched, and the edges of its facets have been blurred by time and wear, which makes me think the stone is not a stone at all but glass. The whole thing is the size of a dime.

I can't discount this ring as being worthless. The inside of the band is stamped "sterling," and underneath the small silver platter that holds the stones an intricate pattern is carved—scrolls and fountain-like flourishes dance around this small, hidden circle. There is a little hole in the center to let light illuminate the blue glass. When I hold it to the sunlight coming through the window, this pinpoint of light looks like a pupil, the circle of blue glass an iris, the white ring of stones a sclera; together they look like a bright blue eye—my grandmother's eye—looking back at me.

I start to fantasize that this ring wields magical powers. If I hold it up to the light, she'll be able to see me. She'll know what I'm doing, and she'll know that I'm thinking of her even though it's been ten years and I've never visited her at Palm Garden. The more I look into this blue glass eye, the more I'm convinced of my fantasy. I put the ring down on my desk, but it's still looking at me. I turn it away, so I can only see the scrollwork carved into its back, the angle of the light falling downward toward the wood of the desk and not into my own frightened face.

Maybe this is a family ring. Maybe it comes from the Old World or from my grandmother's Montreal. Maybe this was a ring she bought as a child and kept all these years. Maybe it was an inheritance from her own grandmother. My father doesn't know, and my grandmother will never tell.

The Book of Wings tells us that if you carve a "hoopo" (a brightly colored European bird) and a sprig of tarragon on an aquamarine, you can call up the dead and question them. But my grandmother will live for another three years, and I have left her aquamarines uncarved. Instead, I have read and studied, theorized and speculated, asked my father a thousand questions and wondered where the truth lies. *The Curious Lore of Precious Stones* claims that "symbolism is always treacherous ground, since there is practically no limit to the correspondences that may be found between . . . impressions and ideas."

But symbolism and stories are all I have. A cat's watchful eye, a prayer for transformation, a wish for safe passage, a desire for new beginnings, a black mirror of speculation, a small kernel of hope. If I have asked for knowledge, I have been given only a pouch of rings. The gods grant wishes in unexpected ways.

Shells

Primer

The gun is heavier than I expected.

We are standing in his living room, the man who is teaching me how to shoot a shotgun and I. I am holding his shotgun, a Remington 12-gauge. He tells me,

Never load the gun until you plan to use it. He tells me,

Keep your finger off the trigger until you plan to pull it. He tells me,

Always point the gun up or away until you plan to shoot it.

The last is the only rule I would have guessed.

My finger wants to be on the trigger even though the gun is unloaded and pointed up and away. The trigger calls to it, but I keep my finger off.

He says, *Stand with one foot a little in front of the other. Bend your front knee. Put the stock in the hollow under your collarbone between your chest and shoulder. Put your cheek against the stock*—so the kick doesn't bruise or break it. *Now you're ready.*

A primer is a preparatory coat on an unpainted surface, an introduction, or the cap that ignites the charge in the cartridge.

It's been thirty years since I've shot a gun, a .22 rifle on my grandparents' farm in Michigan.

But now I'm primed.

Powder

The man who is teaching me how to shoot a shotgun takes a knife from his belt and cuts a shell open for me. We are in a place where men wear knives on their belts.

He cuts through the casing and shows me the parts: the primer, the powder, the wad column, the shot. The powder, he says, is a combustible (able to catch fire and burn easily), not an explosive (able or likely to shatter violently or burst apart).

I think again of *Wuthering Heights*, when Heathcliff and Cathy part, "the gunpowder lay as harmless as sand, because no fire came near to explode it." But then Heathcliff returns, and the fire with him.

I wonder if our powder is still combustible. If it will prove explosive in the end, if the explosion will be the end.

I ask the man who is teaching me how to shoot a shotgun if I can keep this cut-apart shell. He says yes, but first we go outside and he taps the powder out on a slate and makes a fuse from a twist of paper towel. When the powder ignites, it fizzes and crackles but doesn't explode. *When we were kids, we'd write our names it in*, he says.

I thrill as I watch the flames. I don't know if what I smell is the powder or the paper burning.

Wad Column

When the earplugs go in, I can hear my heart beating hard, my breathing loud between nose and ears, everything else far away and quiet. I am not afraid, but I am not my usual self either. Again I feel the heaviness of the gun. I anticipate its kick.

We are in the woods, away from others. The man who is teaching me how to shoot a shotgun sees an owl flying away from the clearing, but I miss it. An owl in the bright afternoon.

I load my first shell and push the fore-end up and back with that iconic sound that cuts through my earplugs. My heart beats harder. Inside the barrel the shell waits—just one—the powder held apart by the wad column, the primer waiting for the pin.

I press my cheek to the stock. I curl my finger around the trigger. I hear my breath, my heart.

The more I wait for the boom and kick, the less expected it is when it comes.

Shot

There are 410 lead pellets in the cartridge I load. When they hit the cardboard box, our target, they leave a hole the size of my fist. I am both pleased and uneasy by the damage I've caused. With the smallest of movements, the box is destroyed.

A projectile is something propelled through the air, especially one thrown as a weapon. I think of what you threw at me: your weight, my words.

The pellets are so small, smaller than a dragée, one of those little silver balls that decorate a cake or cookie. False metal to hide the sweetness. But these pellets are made with lead.

Casing

Before we leave, we pick up the casings, bright red in the dull dead leaves. My cheek is also red. The next day a bruise will show. But for now it is hot, and I am happy, exhilarated, still quivering with the anticipation of something already passed.

The casings hold the shell together, the way a ship's hull keeps the water out, a seed's hull keeps in both shoot and root. The shell casing protects and encloses the powder and the shot until they are ready to burst forth and achieve their desired aim.

I hold a shell in my hand and look at the cardboard box half-shredded on the ground. My thumb, the size of the shell; the hole, the size of your heart.

Camouflet

I pull on my boots and head out. I'm not sure where to, but it doesn't really matter. I am out, and I am walking.

I'm wearing jeans, a black T-shirt, and sunglasses. This is my default. It shouldn't matter what I'm wearing, but it does.

I walk fast, although I am not in a hurry. I am tall with a long stride. I can cover a mile without entirely being aware of it.

Instead, I'm checking the sky, noting clouds. I'm feeling the weather on my face and hands, the sidewalk under my heels. I'm listening as I thread through a crowd or pause at a crosswalk—to conversation, to birds, to traffic's rush, a truck's grumble, the general hum and swell of the city. I smell diesel and spring earth and fresh cut grass, sometimes garbage and sometimes perfume. I see faces and trees and purses and sidewalk and newspapers, a menu listing tapas, a dog with a missing leg, a sticker on the back of a sign that says EYE SOAR. I am looking and walking and looking and walking.

I am a *flâneuse*.

Lauren Elkin, in her book *Flâneuse: Women Walk the City in Paris, New York, Tokyo, Venice, and London*, says that the male of this species, the *flâneur*, is "'one who wanders aimlessly,' was born in the first half of the nineteenth century, in the glass-and-steel-covered *passages* of Paris . . . A figure of masculine privilege and leisure, with time and money and no immediate responsibilities to claim his attention, the *flâneur* . . . [was] an idler, a dawdling observer, usually found in cities."

A *flâneuse* is a female *flâneur*, but her history is a little more complicated. She is a younger concept, since social conventions made it difficult, if not impossible, for women to walk unchaperoned until early in the twentieth century. And she is also in some ways a less stable concept. Luc Sante claims that it is "crucial for the *flâneur* to be functionally invisible," but this is more difficult for women, whose appearance is constantly scrutinized. Someone who is *en flânant*, whether male or female, is the one doing the looking, not the one being looked at. *En flânant* you have agency. You are the subject, never the object.

Wearing what I am wearing—jeans, boots, a dark T-shirt, a drab jacket—it is easy to look without being looked at. At my age, my height, with my build, my particular blend of striking and plain, I am functionally invisible. For me it is a pleasure.

In the early 1830s the writer George Sand, a woman, had a man's overcoat and a pair of boots made for her so she could have the same pleasure—to walk the streets of Paris free to look at whatever she liked. In her autobiography she writes: "I can't express the pleasure my boots gave me . . . With those little iron-shod heels, I was on solid pavement. I flew from one end of Paris to the other. It seemed to me that I could go round the world. And then, my clothes feared nothing. I ran out in every kind of weather, I came home at every sort of hour . . . No one paid attention to me, and no one guessed at my disguise . . . No one knew me, no one looked at me, no one found fault with me; I was an atom lost in that immense crowd."

To be *en flânant* is to be part of a large whole, to blend in with the crowd, to observe it from within, from the psychic distance invisibility allows.

In this way the *flâneuse* is camouflaged. *Camouflage* comes from French street slang, derived from the French *camouflet*, a "whiff of smoke in the face." For George Sand this meant dressing like a man. For me it means dressing plainly. But however she is dressed, the *flâneuse* has an attitude that makes her invisible. She does not call attention to herself because her attention is focused outward. Behind this smoke screen the *flâneuse* walks on, unchallenged.

I strap on sandals and head out. It is summer, bright, the heat relentless, and I am slower, more tentative; I feel exposed. I do not like to feel so bare. I miss my boots. I still wear my jeans—cuffed high in compromise against the heat of a mid-Atlantic August—but I do not put on a skirt or dress. I value my ability to move freely, to move anonymously, androgynously, more than I value staying cool.

I try to get comfortable in these sandals. They are simple, dark brown, a thin T-strap and a loop around my ankle. I try to imagine the person who wears them so I can inhabit her. She is cool, breezy, at ease in the world, wandering through an art museum, having an iced coffee at a café, vaguely window-shopping. This woman is almost me but somehow not. These sandals are too slight, leave me too vulnerable. My shirt—a loose cotton tunic—is a white flag that surrenders my camouflage to the heat. When I come home, I take it all off, kick my sandals to the back of my closet. Next time out I will wear something else.

I slide into flats and head out. These flats are an attempt to wear something other than boots in the summertime. They are an odd hybrid of ballet flat and hiking shoe—the shape feminine, the color bright, the bottom treaded rubber, the top stretchy like a water shoe. I can walk in these flats, move in them, but they are very different from my boots. And they change me.

In these shoes I feel twenty years younger. I become a gamine. I have almost a skip in my step. I look at things—fruits at the farmers market, a little white dog, a man carrying a bouquet of flowers— with more wonder. I am more open when I wear these shoes—and more vulnerable.

Sitting at an outdoor café I notice other *flâneuses* walking by. I admire one's closed-toe sandals and make a note to look for a pair of my own. I see a version of my teenage self in one wearing ripped jeans and Chuck Taylors. I wonder how they feel as they walk through the world, what they are looking at, what they think about it.

I pull on my cowboy boots and head out. I bought these boots with money I made from my writing, and when I wear them, I feel like a writer. I also feel like a woman—instead of simply a person. My usual boots are rather plain, with a rounder toe and a lower heel. These cowboy boots are the closest things to heels I'll wear for anything other than a wedding or a funeral.

We've had a long breaking-in period, these boots and I, but now we are comfortable with each other.

They make me more visible, though—this small alteration to the shape of my foot, the pointed toe, the higher heel. Perhaps I walk differently and that different walk is the pebble thrown into the pond. Sometimes I court these ripples. I wear these boots to readings, to conferences, to parties where other writers often want to joust to show our respective places in the world. In these boots I can step into those stirrups easily, although I prefer to be on foot, walking with less fanfare—and alone.

I pull off my boots and head in. It is autumn and evening, and I am in the vaulted nave of a large church, where a canvas labyrinth has been laid out on the cold stone floor. It is the Chartres labyrinth—not the simpler Cretan one—and you cannot easily see its path without following it with your feet. It is not a maze—there are no dead ends or wrong choices—just one way in, twisting and turning in long half-circles and more tightly coiled ones, until you get to the center. In the center you pause. You can think, pray, or meditate. You can stay there for a second, a minute, or an hour. Then you walk the same path out again.

But it is never quite the same path. The physical route is clear and charted, but the interior journey is not. You might walk in with a question and walk out not with an answer but with a different need or uncertainty; you might walk in with a plea and leave with a plan; you might walk in with a hunger and leave sustained.

There are no distractions—no sidewalks or storefronts or buses or cars. There is just the path and the quiet of the nave. There are other people, but they are looking inward too. You might pass another on her way in or out, but you don't pay attention. You make the way easy for each other, stepping aside or pausing to let them pass, and then you walk on.

I pull on my boots—my usual pair—and head out. It is winter now and dark early, and the streetlights are warm and golden in the clear cold air. I can't help but think of Virginia Woolf's essay "Street Haunting" and how she uses the errand of buying a pencil as an excuse to leave "the solitude of one's own room" and "indulge safely in the greatest pleasure of town life in the winter—rambling the streets of London." I wonder at her use of the word *safely*. What dangers did rambling present? Is she concerned for her physical safety—or does she worry about the ways that walking and looking can destabilize the self?

Woolf does not mention coats or boots or shirts or shoes. She moves through the wintry streets not as a woman, not dressed as a man, but disembodied—"an enormous eye . . . gliding smoothly on the surface," and as it floats, it rests, pauses, and "the brain sleeps perhaps as it looks."

She is an "eye" but not an "I"—the pronoun she uses is *we*. Like George Sand, she becomes an "an atom lost in that immense crowd." Perhaps there is safety in this plurality; there is certainly anonymity and androgyny. We look in store windows. We linger by the Thames. "We halt at the door of a boot shop" but only to look, not to try anything on, not to buy a pair off the shelf or ask to have one made. Instead, Woolf—in the form of an eye, a we—returns to the street, to dip in and out of the lives she passes, the selves she imagines: "It is, in fact, on the stroke of six; it is a winter's evening; we are walking to the Strand to buy a pencil. How, then, are we also on a balcony, wearing pearls in June? . . . Is the true self this which stands on the pavement in January, or that which bends over the balcony in June? Am I here, or am I there? Or is the true self neither this nor that, neither here nor there, but something so varied and wandering that it is only when we give rein to its wishes and let it take its way unimpeded that we are indeed ourselves?"

"Street haunting" can free us from our usual selves. We can let our minds wander through both time and space, trying on and discarding different selves from past, present, and future. But for me, *en flânant* in the twenty-first century, there is another freedom. This is the freedom of haunting without being haunted, of looking without being looked at, of considering, gauging, and wondering without being assessed or appraised myself. This is the freedom of not projecting a self for others to consume but of keeping my true self to myself. My energy is spent in walking and wondering, not absorbing and deflecting. It is like a door that only opens outward, a turnstile, a semipermeable membrane. This is a freedom I value greatly.

As I wander down my own winter street, the streetlamps casting their golden light, the river the Potomac and not the Thames, I feel part of the larger "we," one atom among many. I walk, in my boots and overcoat, and I look out from my layers of anonymity, my invisibility, that whiff of smoke to the face.

I am moving fast, although I am not in a hurry. I'm not sure where to, but it doesn't really matter. I am *en flânant*, following Sand, following Woolf, giving rein to my wandering wishes, heading across town, around the corner, and out of sight.

VI

The Red Thread

Knots

Wood

A knot in wood is the base of a side branch or a dormant bud.

You are my knot.

After we tried, and tried again, and foundered and failed, years grew around the space you left behind, the phantom limb that still itches in certain towns, in summer parks, in late August.

Did the branch die? Is the bud merely dormant? Layers grew, a wedding ring, but the knot remains. If my mind is planed down by time, will you, the knot, fall out?

Cord

One hundred and twenty-eight cubic feet of cut wood is a cord. A long thin flexible string or rope made from several twisted strands is a cord. A length of such material used to fasten or move an object is a cord. An anatomic structure—a spine, an umbilicus—is a cord. An insulated cable that carries an electric current is a cord.

My family is a cord. Flexible, umbilical, insulated, moving, electric.

The word *cord* travels through Middle English and Old French and Latin from the Greek *khorde*, meaning "gut." *Gut* comes from the Old English *guttas*, probably related to *geotan*, "to pour."

My guts pour out, intuition pours in. Four twisted strands, four strings, four notes: a chord.

Muscle

It takes strength to move between opposites, between safety and danger, steeping and swimming, *x* and *y*, love and love.

Muscles break before they build; the fibers stretch until they fray; new cells surge to fill the gaps, and the muscle strengthens.

As a fetus grows, it stretches the uterus so strongly the abdominal muscles part. As a presence grows, it becomes engrained; invoking it becomes a muscle memory.

A knot is a trigger point. A muscle contracts but does not release. The fibers tense and ball. The only cure is touch. Or time.

Speed

To sail you need wind and something it can push against—a sheet, a cloth, a shirt, a leaf. You can sail with the wind or against it, if you know how to navigate currents of both air and water.

A knot is the speed of one nautical mile per hour. When you achieve speed, you leave a wake. You may leave things in your wake—a trail of bubbles, flotsam or jetsam, the past, illusions, people you once were, people you once loved.

The word *leak* comes from the German or Dutch for "lack."

In a wooden ship leaking knotholes are plugged with pitch. Liquid when hot, the pitch hardens as it cools. When it is cold, the knothole is filled. When it is cold, you don't feel the lack.

Shore

Things become lighter in water. A body floats, a ship. An abstraction. Things move fluidly—memory, longing. But always a coast waits, at the horizon or over. A cord pulls. The lightness, the weightlessness, is eventually pulled to shore.

No one knows why a certain sandpiper is called a "knot." The red knot breeds in the Arctic and winters in the southern hemisphere, the distance between a vertical ocean.

Sandpipers live on the edge, in the littoral zone, between sea and shore. The mermaids sing, the sirens call, beauty masking danger, desire drowning sense, but the sandpiper is silent. It tacks back and forth, skitters out of reach, testing, never caught.

A shipwreck becomes a pile of wood to salvage. A dead branch becomes lumber or kindling or mulch.

No knot. No hole. A different set of cords to pluck and pull and bind.

69 Inches of Thread, Scarlet and Otherwise

> There's the scarlet thread of murder running through
> the colourless skein of life, and our duty is to unravel it,
> and isolate it, and expose every inch of it.
>
> Sherlock Holmes, *A Study in Scarlet*

1. *Scarlet*: ORIGIN Middle English (originally denoting any brightly colored cloth).

2. When I was fifteen, I bought a bright red dress to wear to my friend's confirmation.

3. At the party he had the DJ play "Lady in Red" and asked me to dance.

4. Everyone looked at us, me hot with power but otherwise cool.

5. About the same age I started reading the Sherlock Holmes novels.

6. *Scarlet*: from Late Latin *sigillatus*, "decorated with small images."

7. I had a notebook then, what I might call a commonplace book now, where I wrote song lyrics I liked and poems and glued in black-and-white photographs and drew vines and stars and spirals in the margins.

8. One of the poems I would recite to myself again and again over the years, when the shine left a romance, was Mary Carolyn Davies's "Rust":

9.

> Iron, left in the rain
>> And fog and dew
> With rust is covered.—Pain
>> Rusts into beauty, too.
>
> I know full well that this is so:
> —I had a heartbreak long ago.

10. Davies was born in the 1890s, one hundred years before I found her poem but just a few years before Arthur Conan Doyle set Sherlock Holmes loose in the world.

11. When we first encounter Holmes—*meet* feels like too friendly a verb—he is trying to devise a test for human hemoglobin, the iron-containing protein within red blood cells.

12. With this knowledge Holmes can analyze bloodstains at the scene of a crime.

13. *Scarlet*: . . . from *sigillum*, "small image."

14. Despite my success with the red dress, I did not court attention.

15. I wanted to be the observer, not the observed.

16. I liked to keep secrets. Your picture, cut from the church directory, in a locket. Your photograph, stolen from the school darkroom, in my favorite paperback. Some small part of you hidden in some small part of me until I could make it real.

17. When I was half again as young, I read *Harriet the Spy* and filled my own composition notebooks with observations about my family, my friends, neighbors, and strangers.

18. I thought I would be a spy.

19. Instead, I became an essayist.

20. *Thread*: ORIGIN Old English *thrǣd* (noun), of Germanic origin; related to Dutch *draad* and German *Draht*, also to the verb *throw*.

21. Sherlock Holmes was only undone once, and by a woman.

22. I have undone several boys and several men, thrown them over—never casually but with the same relentless trajectory. And several have thrown me.

23. But if you're not going to tie your knot to another, what else is to be done?

24. Besides, a metaphorical broken heart rarely kills.

25. Alternate definitions of *murder* range from . . .

26. . . . a very difficult or unpleasant task or experience (when no would not be taken as an answer) . . .

27. . . . to punish severely or be very angry with (when you said, "People who love each other don't treat each other that way") . . .

28. . . . to conclusively defeat (when Irene Adler—"*the* woman"—escapes from Sherlock Holmes and disappears) . . .

29. . . . to spoil by lack of skill or knowledge (when I didn't know how to eat a tamale and made to bite the husk, when I gouged the brie instead of taking the rind, when I spit the scotch back into the glass, when my salary wasn't enough, when my not-caring about these things was too much).

30. And the shame of it—the hot blush of ignorance and innocence, especially when provoked by desire.

31. What can be told from the stain of blood across the cheek?

32. And how much should be told?

33. Must every inch be unraveled and exposed?

34. *Unravel*: ORIGIN Late Middle English (in the sense of "entangle, confuse"), probably from Dutch *ravelen*, "fray out, tangle."

35. A relationship can unravel, a lie, a pose, a mask, a front.

36. Unraveling causes confusion, but confusion can also cause unraveling.

37. "There are two kinds of women: those who knit and those who unravel . . . Once I see the loose thread, I am undone. It's over before I have even asked myself the question: Do I actually want to destroy this?"—from the essay "The Unravelers" by Stephanie Danler

38. I have unraveled relationships, lies, poses, masks, fronts.

39. I have unraveled medieval texts and Renaissance plays, nineteenth-century novels and twenty-first-century essays.

40. I have knit myself to unravelers and been unraveled myself.

41. I have been an unraveler of knitters.

42. Does unraveling always destroy?

43. Can magic survive scrutiny?

44. Or is there always a trick, a mirror, a misdirection to be exposed?

45. *Skein*: a length of thread or yarn, loosely coiled and knotted.

46. *Skein*: a tangled or complicated arrangement, state, or situation.

47. *Skein*: a flock of wild geese or swans in flight, typically in a V-shaped formation.

48. *Astonishment*: the sound of wild geese flying over me, in my kayak in the middle of the lake, the way they broke the stillness with their loud and throbbing wing beats, the way the sound itself seemed to

propel them through the air, the way the dip of my paddle into the water after they left felt so weak and feeble as I returned to shore, returned to you, thinking only of when I, too, would fly away.

49. But don't forget: pain rusts into beauty too.

50. I am 69 inches long if I'm lying on a bed, across the back seat of a 1980 Buick Century station wagon, on a library floor, on a stack of patio cushions, in a loft, in a church basement, on the roof of a beach house, on a press box.

51. I am the same 69 inches if I'm telling the truth.

52. "Tell all the truth but tell it slant / Success in Circuit lies."—Emily Dickinson

53. Emily Dickinson died the same year Sherlock Holmes began.

54. Holmes might have used circuitous means to get at the truth, but the truth he sought was straight.

55. The evidence told the story.

56. The evidence didn't lie.

57. Scarlet thread embroidered an *A*, stitched together a dress, sewed together shoes, fixed the seams of a tent, secured the lines of a flag.

58. The stitches in my face after you crashed the motorcycle as well as my hopes for us were blue. But it was a red thread of desire that had me on the back of that bike, holding onto your waist as you couldn't hold the curve, as the barbed wire fence opened its own red threads across my cheek, stole my blush, marked me for life.

59. *Isolate*: ORIGIN mid-eighteenth century, from French *isolé*, from Italian *isolato*, from Late Latin *insulatus*, "made into an island," from Latin *insula*, "island."

60. Sometimes it is easier to see something in isolation, when there is nothing near to compete or compare.

61. A magnifying glass can work to bring one small thing, one small place, into looming focus while everything around it blurs into oblivion.

62. *A Study in Scarlet* was the first detective novel to feature a magnifying glass as a means of investigation.

63. In the Magnificat, in the Gospel of Luke, Mary says, "My soul magnifies the Lord, and my spirit rejoices in God."

64. A piece of glass, a joyous soul, a lover's gaze, a writer's mind.

65. *Expose:* ORIGIN Late Middle English, from Old French *exposer* . . . influenced by Latin *expositus*, "put or set out," and Old French *poser*, "to place."

66. When a crime is exposed, it is set out for all to see, often against the criminal's desire.

67. But when a writer is exposed through her own writing, she is putting stories, ideas, settings, and feelings into place. Knitting them together. The scarlet thread runs through, and the skein becomes brighter for it.

68. It is intentional. Calculated. Almost Holmesian.

69. Most of the time.

On Silence

The Quiet Car

The quiet car on this Amtrak train, traveling along the Northeast Corridor, is not very quiet. There is the sound of the train itself, of crinkly bags and wrappers, music through headphones—the drum beats coming through tight and tinny, the shock of the door opening, a louder sound of wheels on track, occasionally muted conversation between two seat mates.

But these are all sounds that can be tuned out. What is more difficult to ignore is half a conversation—one talker on a cell phone, overcompensating for a questionable connection, loudly proclaiming to whoever is on the other end what is painfully obvious to the rest of us: "I'm on the train."

We seek out the quiet car because we want our ears to be our own and not used as a hole for other people's noise. John Biguenet, in his book *Silence*, claims that this kind of quiet has become "a luxury that—like most luxuries—begins to feel less like a luxury and more a necessity the more often one indulges in its pleasures." Once I discovered the quiet car, I have always sought it out.

But I have always sought out silence in all its varied forms: the absence of sound, the absence of speech, the abstention from speech. But silence feels to me less like an absence and more like a presence. Sara Maitland tries to reframe it this way in *A Book of Silence*, claiming that silence "is 'outwith language.' 'Outwith' is a wonderful Scottish word for which standard English appears to have no exact equivalent—outwith means 'outside of,' 'not within the circumference of something else.' 'Without' is necessarily negative and suggests that something is lacking."

But *outwith* suggests a different position, a change of perspective, an outside stance looking in, at the edge, perhaps eavesdropping, perhaps listening, or perhaps content to be in a place outside sound and words, a place of silence.

The Museum

The museum is not as quiet as I would expect either.

In the East Building of the National Gallery of Art, on the very top floor, is a room dedicated to the work of Mark Rothko. The walls are white, the floor blond wood. Below me a bench, above me a lattice of skylights. Around me are ten iconic Rothkos.

For a few minutes I am the only one here. For a few minutes it is almost quiet. I hear only the whir of the air conditioner and a set of automatic doors sliding open and closed a few rooms away. The paintings are, as John Berger writes, "silent and still." They draw me into their vivid colors—ochers and umbers and teals and plums. They set my imagination spinning with their relentless abstraction—rectangular shapes, color on color: what does this represent, what does this mean, I don't know, I want to know, I can't know. Rothko himself enjoyed the idea that his paintings could not be translated into words. "Silence is so accurate," he said.

But all too soon the silence around me is broken. There are footfalls and sneaker squeaks on the hardwood floor. Children's voices muffled by their own reverb. A guard's voice cutting through a walkie-talkie, followed by even louder bursts of static. The sharp slap of a dropped booklet. Conversations in English, French, and German.

I sit on the bench and keep looking at the paintings. People come and go, but they are easy to tune out. Then I am alone again.

At last, I think, I can be silent with these silent paintings. I start to consider John Berger's claim that "original paintings are silent and still in a sense that information never is . . . for in the original silence and stillness permeate the actual material, the paint, in which one follows the traces of the painter's immediate gestures." I start to see brushstrokes within the colors, a little bleed, a faint drip, and I feel the distance closing between me looking and Rothko painting.

But then, in my bag, my phone buzzes. It is a text telling me that my AutoPay has gone through and I have another month of unlimited minutes for more talk, more texts. More information moving. More words to fill the silence. I turn my phone off, but someone else has already come into the room talking loudly of lunch plans.

The Library

The Main Reading Room of the Library of Congress is neither silent nor quiet. From the hallway I can hear many diffuse voices talking—a tour. From closer I can hear people typing, people turning pages, the occasional echoing cough or sneeze. Setting a pen down on this wooden desk is very, very loud. So is a door opening and closing behind me. There is an almost audible energy here—many people thinking, reading, writing.

Even the visuals of the room feel loud. They command attention even in their silence. As a new reader here, I can't help but play the tourist, gawk at the domed ceiling, at the statues looking down from the highest level—Greeks, Romans, Elizabethans. Later I learn that there are sixteen of these bronze statues (including Plato, Columbus, Shakespeare, and Newton) as well as eight plaster figures representing spheres of civilized life and thought: Religion, Commerce, History, Art, Philosophy, Poetry, Law, and Science. Beneath them we read our books, take our notes, make our copies, and listen to the echoes of tour guides, the turning pages, the dropped pencils.

In these ways the library is not silent at all.

In other ways its silence is deafening.

Tillie Olsen writes, "Literary history and the present are dark with silences: some the silences for years by our acknowledged great; some silences hidden; some the ceasing to publish after one work appears; some the never coming to book form at all." This is the first sentence of her book *Silences*, which explores creative silences that are an "unnatural thwarting of what struggles to come into being, but cannot." She writes of the working class, people of color, and women.

I look up at the statues ringing this room. I see Shakespeare and think of the way Virginia Woolf imagined the life of his sister. I see Plato and wonder what philosophies his slaves would have shared. I think of the people who are not in this room, the people to whom Olsen dedicated her book: "our silenced people, century after century their beings consumed in the hard, everyday essential work of maintaining human life. Their art, which still they made—as their other contributions— anonymous; refused respect, recognition; lost . . . [And] those of us (few yet in number, for the way is punishing), their kin and descendants who begin to emerge into more flowered and rewarded use of our selves in ways denied to them;—and by our achievement bearing witness to what was (and still is) being lost, silenced." When will a library of this magnitude, this grandeur, feature them and their work as well?

In his book *Silence* John Biguenet claims that we can't navigate in silence. He quotes a scientist who explains that "you orient your- self . . . through sounds you hear when you walk. In [a completely silent] anechoic chamber you don't have any cues. You take away the perceptual cues that allow you to balance and maneuver."

We need to be able to hear versions of our own voices as we walk through the world—not just Paul in the Gospels but all the Marys and Marthas too, not just Jefferson in his study but Sally Hemmings as well, and not only Virginia Woolf but the Nellies in the kitchen and the dropouts from Slade and the boy on the corner selling news- papers. The members of the working class, people of color, women. On the shelves of the library if not also cast in bronze.

The Cabin

I came to this small dark cabin in the Blue Ridge Mountains to write in solitude, but I was not prepared for the silence.

A bird landing in the leaves outside sounds like a charging bear. Inside, turning the page of a book sounds like the first crack of thunder. I stop moving because I make too much noise, and with my body stilled, my mind begins to wander. The silence is already unnerving by dusk, but when I turn out the lights to sleep, it is not only silent but black. I have entered the void.

I see every hour on the clock. Each noise jolts me—an oak tassel falling on the tin roof, the creaking of the shifting timbers, even my own stomach growling or the faint whistle of air through my nose. Sometime between three and four in the morning I remember that sleep deprivation is a form of torture. Then I start to hear faint conversations and music in the distance, even though I know that I am the only human being for miles. After four o'clock I remember Tim O'Brien's "How to Tell a True War Story" and the radio men who were ordered into complete silence in the Vietnamese jungle and how they started hearing cocktail party chatter and chamber music and Buddhist chanting and full-scale operas out there in the silent, seething dark. It was the mountains talking, the rock, the landscape itself. I could hear the same in my mountains. Or was I going crazy too? At five thirty the faint outline of trees becomes dark against an anvil sky; dawn is not far behind. At last.

Later I would read about Sara Maitland's experience with silence and isolation, how she, too, felt an extraordinary intensification of physical sensations, how she heard voices, how she felt "unskinned" and—almost—a sense of madness. But then, alone in that dark cabin, I could only feel myself coming unhinged.

The next day is beautiful—clear blue skies, bustling green woods, birdsong and breeze. I am tired, but I sit on the porch and read; I sit at my desk and write. But then the day wanes, and the outline of the trees grows flush against the darkening sky. The tin roof creaks as it cools; my chair squeaks as I shift. I give up and get ready for bed.

I turn out the lights in the kitchen and then in the middle of the cabin; one bedside lamp still burns. When I turn back the covers, a cave cricket springs out at me. I start to tear up, sitting in the bed, shivering, the bedside lamp now out, a flashlight clutched in my fist. Through the ringing silence in my ears I start to hear a faint, whirring moan. An insect? I click on the flashlight and scan the cabin—nothing but shadows, worse than the dark. I get up and turn on the light. Still nothing. The invisible moaning continues. I cannot spend another sleepless night here. I reach for the phone and book a room at a nearby retreat center. Within minutes I am driving away.

"You need deep roots for that cabin," a friend tells me later. "Or you have to grow them fast." I nod but then wonder. Maybe I don't have deep roots. And maybe I had missed my chance of growing them when I pulled up and fled. I hadn't realized the difference between quiet and silence, between solitude and isolation.

I want to try again—but not yet.

The Cemetery

Arlington Cemetery is iconic—the uniform rows of uniform headstones stretch out in ways that feel both endless and eternal. But it is not very quiet—at least not on a summer afternoon. Visitors flood the pedestrian paths. They are relatively subdued but not silent. They are mostly tourists—respectful tourists but still tourists. Most are here to see a sight, not to visit a grave. And so am I.

There are soft high-pitched crickets and the occasional harsher grinding cicadas. Planes fly overhead, and at noon a bell tolls twelve. Some birds take a bath in a little stream. Cheeps and chitters.

But then I hear a brass band in the distance. Its warm notes are distorted—is it "Nearer My God to Thee"?—but the drumbeat that follows is an unmistakable dirge. I walk up a small rise and see them through tree leaves on a road below: marines in red and blue, four white horses pulling a caisson, and there—the flag-draped casket. They march out of view, but later I hear three unmistakable rifle shots. I look at the graves where I am standing and think about how each contains a body, a life now ended, and how each was buried here, with perhaps the same ceremony or perhaps none. I can barely imagine the way most of them died, their wartime deaths the exact opposite of this, their final grassy resting place.

My hometown cemetery is much smaller, much older, and much more quiet. I don't know anyone who is buried there, but I visit it anyway. In the graveyard close to the church are families who died in the 1700s. The man who built the house I grew up in is buried there. Farther down the hill are grassless graves so new they don't yet have a marker.

It is quiet but not silent. I can hear the wind ruffling the oak leaves, a cicada drone rising and falling, a distant mower, closer crickets, occasional birds, occasional cars, and once one loud crow. I think about the oblique stories on these headstones, how they serve as tiny biographies. I'm especially struck by the poignancy of the ones that list the exact lifespan of the person lying beneath—"67 years 11 mos & 22 days"—because each day, even the twenty-second, mattered to the man who lived them.

In *When Women Were Birds*, Terry Tempest Williams's mother is dying. "I am leaving you all my journals," she tells her daughter. "But you must promise me that you will not look at them until after I am gone."

Less than a month later, on the night of a full moon, Williams feels it is time.

"I opened the first journal. It was empty. I opened the second journal. It was empty. I opened the third. It, too, was empty, as was the fourth, the fifth, the sixth—shelf after shelf after shelf, all my mother's journals were blank." The next five pages look like this:

The ongoing silence after death is total. We might find an old letter, a note in the margins of a long-closed book, a voicemail saved to be listened to time and time again, but there is no continuing conversation. The graves of Arlington stand mute aside from their names and dates. A civilian grave might say more. Keats's says, "Here Lies One Whose Name Was Writ in Water." Emily Dickinson's says, "Called back." But Hamlet's last words resonate for both the one dying as well as for the living left behind: "The rest is silence."

The Monastery

My first morning at the abbey, my alarm goes off at three. I feel like I've barely slept, but I pull on the sweater and jeans I laid out the night before, brush my teeth, wipe my face with a damp cloth, grab my coat, and head out into the frosty dark. The cold air wakes me up sharp. The abbey chapel is only a five-minute walk away, but as my flashlight beam bobs in the dark, I feel uneasy. Other retreatants may follow, but for now I'm the only soul on the road between two vast pastures. The sky gleams with stars.

When I slip into the chapel, it is dark. A candle burns at the very back of the church, and a dim light shines over one of the doors that leads to the cloister. A monk sits silently in the front row as I slide into a back pew. The nylon of my winter coat whispers every time I move, and I quickly settle with my back straight, my hands in my lap, and my feet on the floor. The only sound is my breathing, and even that begins to quiet.

It seems like a long time before others arrive. Monks in white robes come in from the side doors, some dipping a finger in the holy water and making the sign of the cross, all bowing to the altar before taking their place in the choir. Then a few retreatants come through the door behind me and settle into the pews. A plush rope separates the monks' pews from ours.

A bell rings, and the monks stand. The service is simple—a series of chanted psalms and two readings. I try to keep my head from lolling and jerk awake when the chanting fades and then suddenly sounds like a shout. I try to stay focused. I try not to think about the narrow bed that waits for me in my dark room and resolve to stay awake, as the monks do, until Lauds, hours later.

When the service ends, most of the monks return to the cloister, but two sit in the pews reserved for them. I want to stay longer, but I feel funny being the only retreatant left alone with the monks; I don't want to intrude. So I slip out as quietly as I can and walk back to the retreat house, hunching my shoulders against the cold, stopping only twice to look up at the layers of stars above.

Back in my room it is four o'clock. I take a long hot shower with sandalwood soap and then settle in to read until Lauds at seven. The monks pull their hoods up during this time to symbolize the embrace of God, but I put on a down vest and a scarf for warmth.

The abbey is a place of silence and, through that silence, solitude within the community. Those who come for a retreat at the abbey are asked to keep a personal rule of silence during their stay. You don't need to be totally silent—early in the week some people break the rule to say "Thank you" when something is passed, or to ask if the kitchen worker needs help, or to offer to share a flashlight's beam on the dark walk to Compline. But soon even these few sentences are reduced to gestures—a nod, a set of raised eyebrows, or simply the assumption that something needed is to be shared.

At mealtimes we don't talk, although we don't eat in silence. For the first few nights music is played—the kind of synthesized string-and-piano music you might hear at a Chinese restaurant. Then one night, with no warning or explanation, the music changes to happy baroque. Whatever the music is, we accompany it only with the scrapings of silverware on melamine plates.

I love the silence, the absence of speech. I love not having to make small talk that can turn large fast—what I do for a living, what brings me to the abbey, what I hope to find here. I don't have to reveal that I am a writer interested in silence, or confess that I don't exactly know what I am doing here but am enjoying the process—slowly and quietly—of finding out.

Outside my window it is still dark. A little after six the dawn will bring a weak gray light, but until then it is black and quiet.

Years later I will think of this night, and my night at the cabin in the Blue Ridge Mountains. I will wonder if I would have been comforted by the memory of those monks keeping vigils through the night. I will think of the monastery's graveyard with its simple white crosses and how much smaller it is than the acres of Arlington, although the monks and soldiers beneath now share the same long death. I will think of the statues looking down on the library, the Rothkos hanging wordless in the gallery, the journals blank on the shelf.

But for now I pull a twist of scarf over my head and return to my book, my room quiet except for the sounds I make in it, the candle still and always burning at the back of the church, the vault of the sky above us still dense with silent stars.

Devotional

Matins.

Midnight is too obvious an hour. We sleep through it and faintly wake at odd times instead—1:13, 3:35. These are the hours when I reach for you, forgetting that you sleep now in another's bed, and my dumb hand will find only cool sheet and cooler air. This is the hour of the radiator's hiss, the mouse in the wall.

Lauds.

At dawn the mockingbird breaks into my sleep, sings car alarms and other songs about stealing that have been stolen from other birds. Is it the cuckoo who lays its egg in another's nest? I pull the pillow over my head, muffling sound and thought.

Prime.

By this first hour of undeniable daylight I can no longer pretend to sleep. More birds make a mockery of my efforts. Sometimes the hardest thing is to stand up, go vertical, get straight. I stand.

Terce.

Outside the window the loblolly pine bends in the wind. I move things around the kitchen, cup to counter, egg to plate. Inside a boiling, outside a break. On the radio a love song. I'm pining too.

Sext.

This is the hour of taxicabs and airports, of the dinghy pushed away
from the dock, of cattails and waterweeds and all the currents that
pull you away from me. This is the hour of waiting, for arrivals and
reunion, for the oar to send the surface trembling, the rod to quiver
with the longed-for bite.

None.

You once told me that cold hands are the body's way of protecting itself, drawing blood from limb to keep the vital center safe. But now my vital center is no longer part of my body, and I sit with this coffee cup between my palms, warming what is cold with loss. I hold this heat in my hands.

Vespers.

In the evening, storm clouds and swallowtails. I am the cloud you cut through with your keen wings. I am also the tail swallowed.

Compline.

At night, before retiring, I wonder how many hours have I spent waiting for you to appear. Have these hours added up to a day? How many days? And how many more? Regardless, I remain devoted. No vote, no choice. Just you.

Acknowledgments

Plenteous thanks to my family (past and present), Karen Askarinam, and Sarah Ann Winn; thanks, too, for the vectors given by André Aciman, Pat Hoy, Sarah Einstein, Dinty W. Moore, and Patrick Madden.

Many thanks to the wonderful Virginia Center for the Creative Arts, Hambidge Center for the Creative Arts and Sciences, Weymouth Center for the Arts and Humanities, Sundress Academy for the Arts, the Millay Colony for the Arts (and the MidAtlantic Arts Foundation for awarding me a fellowship to attend), Vermont Studio Center, and Wildacres. Thanks, too, to the District of Columbia Public Library and to Labyrinth Books in Princeton, New Jersey (where spending an afternoon browsing their shelves will make you feel halfway to getting an advanced degree).

Thanks to the District of Columbia Commission on the Arts and Humanities for awarding me an Arts and Humanities Fellowship.

Thanks to the University of Nebraska Press.

And many thanks to you.

The following essays were previously published, sometimes in different form:

"The Split": *Passages North* 31, no. 1 (2009–10).
"Mirror Glimpses": *Emrys Journal* 26 (2009). It won the journal's Nonfiction Prize.
"Elegy for Dracula": *Shenandoah* 64, no. 1, Noir (October 2014).

"Ambush": as "War Wear from a Dangerous Liaison" in the Modern Love column of the *New York Times*, November 16, 2008.

"Leaving the Island": *Mothering Through the Darkness: Women Open Up About the Postpartum Experience*, ed. Jessica Smock and Stephanie Sprenger (She Writes Press, 2015).

"Behind the Caves": *The Rumpus*, September 16, 2014.

"Marked": *Brain, Child Magazine* (online), February 2013.

"The Heart as a Torn Muscle": *Brevity*, no. 48 (January 2015). It was also a Notable Essay in *The Best American Essays 2016*.

"What of the Raven, What of the Dove?": *Rappahannock Review* 2, no. 3 (August 2015).

"Assemblage": *Creative Nonfiction* 66 (Winter 2018).

"The Sparkling Future": *Superstition Review* 11 (Spring 2013).

"Widow Fantasies": *Delmarva Review* 7 (October 2014).

"On Looking": *Massachusetts Review* 48, no. 2 (Summer 2007).

"The Ownership of Memory": as "Stonewall Jackson's Arm" in the *Virginia Quarterly Review*'s blog, May 2, 2013.

"69 Inches of Thread, Scarlet and Otherwise": *Nonbinary Review*, July 2016.

"Devotional": Red Bird Chapbooks, 2017.

Bibliography

Berger, John. *Ways of Seeing*. New York: Penguin Books, 1977.

Biguenet, John. *Silence*. New York: Bloomsbury Academic, 2015.

Brontë, Emily. *Wuthering Heights*. London: Everyman's Library, 1998.

Cohen, Ethan, and Joel Cohen, dirs. *No Country for Old Men*. Film. Los Angeles: Miramax Films, 2007.

Coppola, Francis Ford, dir. *Bram Stoker's Dracula*. Film. Culver City CA: Columbia Pictures, 1992.

Cunningham, Michael. *The Hours*. New York: Picador, 2000.

Daldry, Stephen, dir. *The Hours*. Film. Los Angeles: Paramount Pictures, 2002.

Danler, Stephanie. "The Unravelers." *Paris Review*, September 8, 2015. https://www.theparisreview.org/blog/2015/09/08/the-unravelers/.

Davies, Mary Carolyn. "Rust." In *The New Poetry: An Anthology of Twentieth-Century Verse in English*, edited by Harriet Monroe and Alice Corbin Henderson. New York: Macmillan, 1930.

Defoe, Daniel. *Robinson Crusoe*. London: Penguin Classics, 2003.

Dickinson, Emily. "Tell all the truth but tell it slant." In *The Poems of Emily Dickinson: Reading Edition*. Cambridge: Belknap Press of Harvard University Press, 1998.

Didion, Joan. *The Year of Magical Thinking*. New York: Knopf, 2005.

Doyle, Arthur Conan. *A Study in Scarlet*. Mineola NY: Dover, 2003.

Elkin, Lauren. *Flâneuse: Women Walk the City in Paris, New York, Tokyo, Venice, and London*. New York: Farrar, Straus and Giroux, 2016.

Forster, E. M. *Howards End*. London: Penguin Classics, 2001.

Homer. *The Iliad*. Translated by Robert Fagles. London: Penguin Classics, 1998.

Khayyam, Omar. "The Rubaiyat of Omar Khayyam [excerpt]." Translated by Edward Fitzgerald. Academy of American Poets. https://www.poets.org/poetsorg/poem/rubaiyat-omar-khayyam-excerpt.

Kunz, George Frederick. *The Curious Lore of Precious Stones*. Mineola NY: Dover, 1971.

Laclos, Pierre Choderlos de. *Les Liaisons dangereuses*. Oxford: Oxford University Press, 2008.

Lee, Hermione. *Virginia Woolf*. New York: Vintage Books, 1999.

Maitland, Sara. *A Book of Silence*. Berkeley CA: Counterpoint, 2009.

McCabe, Mitch, dir. *Playing the Part*. Film. Boston: First Run Features, 1995.

Montaigne, Michel de. "Of Practice." In *The Complete Works*. Translated by Donald M. Frame. New York: Knopf, 2003.

Nuland, Sherwin B. *How We Die: Reflections on Life's Final Chapter*. New York: Knopf, 1994.

Olsen, Tillie. *Silences*. 1978. Reprint, New York: The Feminist Press, 2003.

Renault, Mary. *The Charioteer: A Novel*. 1953. Reprint, New York: Vintage, 2003.

Shelley, Mary. *Frankenstein, or, The Modern Prometheus: The 1818 Text*. Oxford: Oxford University Press, 1998.

Shields, Carol. "Mirrors." In *The Collected Stories*. Toronto: Random House Canada, 2004.

Stoker, Bram. *Dracula*. Edited by Nina Auerbach and David J. Skal. Norton Critical Editions. New York: Norton, 1996.

Williams, Terry Tempest. *When Women Were Birds: Fifty-Four Variations on Voice*. New York: Sarah Crichton Books, 2012.

Woolf, Virginia. "Professions for Women." In *The Death of the Moth and Other Essays*. Web edition. University of Adelaide. https://ebooks.adelaide.edu.au/w/woolf/virginia/w91d/chapter27.html.

———. "Street Haunting." In *The Art of the Personal Essay: An Anthology from the Classical Era to the Present*, edited by Philip Lopate. New York: Anchor Books, 1995.

———. *A Writer's Diary*. Edited by Leonard Woolf. New York: Harcourt Brace & Co., 1982.